The Old Road

by Hilaire Belloc

ON THE ROAD AND THE FASCINATION OF ANTIQUITY

There are primal things which move us. Fire has the character of a free companion that has travelled with us from the first exile; only to see a fire, whether he need it or no, comforts every man. Again, to hear two voices outside at night after a silence, even in crowded cities, transforms the mind. A Roof also, large and mothering, satisfies us here in the north much more than modern necessity can explain; so we built in beginning: the only way to carry off our rains and to bear the weight of our winter snows. A Tower far off arrests a man's eye always: it is more than a break in the sky-line; it is an enemy's watch or the rallying of a defence to whose aid we are summoned. Nor are these emotions a memory or a reversion only as one crude theory might pretend; we craved these things—the camp, the refuge, the sentinels in the dark, the hearth—before we made them; they are part of our human manner, and when this civilisation has perished they will reappear.

Of these primal things the least obvious but the most important is The Road. It does not strike the sense as do those others I have mentioned; we are slow to feel its influence. We take it so much for granted that its original meaning escapes us. Men, indeed, whose pleasure it is perpetually to explore even their own country on foot, and to whom its every phase of climate is delightful, receive, somewhat tardily, the spirit of The Road. They feel a meaning in it; it grows to suggest the towns upon it, it explains its own vagaries, and it gives a unity to all that has arisen along its way. But for the mass The Road is silent; it is the humblest and the most subtle, but, as I have said, the greatest and the most original of the spells which we inherit from the earliest pioneers of our race. It was the most imperative and the first of our necessities. It is older than building and than wells; before we were quite men we knew it, for the animals still have it to-day; they seek their food and their drinking-places, and, as I believe, their assemblies, by known tracks which they have made.

It is easy to re-create in oneself to-day a sense of what the Road means to living things on land: it is easy to do it even in this crowded country. Walk, for instance, on the neglected Pennines along the watershed of England, from Malham Tarn, say, to Ribblehead, or from Kirkby Stephen up along the crest to Crossfell and so to Alston, and you will learn at once what follows on an untouched soil from the absence of a track—of a guide. One ravine out of the many radiating from a summit will lead to the one valley you seek; take another stream and you are condemned at last to traverse mountains to repair the error. In a fog or at night, if one has not such a path, there is nothing to help one but the lay of the snow or the trend of the vegetation under the last gale. In climbing, the summit is nearly always hidden, and nothing but a track will save you from false journeys. In descent it alone will save you a precipice or an unfordable stream. It knows upon which side an obstacle can be passed, where there is firm land in a morass, and where there is the best going; sand or rock—dry soil. It will find what nothing but long experiment can find for an individual traveller, the precise point in a saddle or neck where approach is easiest from either side, and everywhere the Road, especially the very early Road, is wiser than it seems to be. It reminds one of those old farmers who do not read, and whom we think at first unreasoning in their curious and devious ways, but whom, if we watch closely, we shall find doing all their work just in that way which infinite time has taught the country-side.

Thus I know an old man in Sussex who never speaks but to say that everything needs rest. Land, he says, certainly; and also he believes iron and wood. For this he is still ridiculed, but what else are the most learned saying now? And I know a path in the Vosges which, to the annoyance of those who travel by it, is irrational: it turns sharp northward and follows under a high ridge, instead of directly crossing it: some therefore leave it and lose all their pains, for, if you will trust to that path you will find it crosses the ridge at last at the only place where, on the far side, it is passable at all; all before and beyond that point is a little ledge of precipice which no one could go down.

More than rivers and more than mountain chains, roads have moulded the political groups of men. The Alps with a mule-track across them are less of a barrier than fifteen miles of forest or rough land separating one from that track. Religions, which are the principal formers of mankind, have followed the roads only, leaping from city to city and leaving the 'Pagani,' in the villages off the road, to a later influence. Consider the series Jerusalem, Antioch, Ephesus, Athens, and the Appian Way: Rome, all the tradition of the Tuscan highway, the Ligurian coast, Marseilles and Lyons. I have read in some man's book that the last link of that chain was the river Rhone; but this man can never have tried to pull a boat upon the Rhone up-stream. It was the Road that laid the train. The Mass had reached Lyons before, perhaps, the last disciple of the apostles was dead: in the Forez, just above, four hundred years later, there were most probably offerings at night to the pagan gods of those sombre and neglected hills.

And with religions all that is built on them: letters, customs, community of language and idea, have followed the Road, because humanity, which is the matter of religion, must also follow the road it has made. Architecture follows it, commerce of course, all information: it is even so with the poor thin philosophies, each in its little day drifts, for choice, down a road.

The sacredness which everywhere attaches to The Road has its sanction in all these uses, but especially in that antiquity from which the quality of things sacred is drawn: and with the mention of the word 'antiquity' I may explain another desire which led me to the study I have set down in this book: not only did I desire to follow a road most typical of all that roads have been for us in western Europe, but also to plunge right into the spirit of the oldest monument of the life men led on this island: I mean the oldest of which a continuous record remains.

A ROAD MOST TYPICAL OF ALL THAT ROADS HAVE BEEN FOR US

To study something of great age until one grows familiar with it and almost to live in its time, is not merely to satisfy a curiosity or to establish aimless truths: it is rather to fulfil a function whose appetite has always rendered History a necessity. By the recovery of the Past, stuff and being are added to us; our lives which, lived in the present only, are a film or surface, take on body—are lifted into one dimension more. The soul is fed. Reverence and knowledge and security and the love of a good land—all these are increased or given by the pursuit of this kind of learning. Visions or intimations are confirmed. It is excellent to see perpetual agony and failure perpetually breeding the only enduring things; it is excellent to see the crimes we know ground under the slow wheels whose ponderous advance we can hardly note during the flash of one human life. One may say that historical learning grants men glimpses of life completed and a whole; and such a vision should be the chief solace of whatever is mortal and cut off imperfectly from fulfilment.

Now of all that study the chief charm lies in mere antiquity. No one truly loves history who is not more exalted according to the greater age of the new things he finds. Though things are less observable as they are farther away, yet their appeal is directly increased by such a distance in a manner which all know though none can define it. It is not illusion; perhaps an ultimate reality stands out when the details are obscured. At any rate it is the appeal which increases as we pass further from the memories of childhood, or from the backward vision of those groups of mountain which seem to rise higher and more awfully into the air as we abandon them across the plains. Antiquity of that degree conveys—I cannot pretend to say how—echoes which are exactly attuned to whatever is least perishable in us. After the present and manifold voice of Religion to which these echoes lead, and with which in a sense they merge, I know of nothing more nobly answering the perpetual questioning of a man. Nor of all the vulgar follies about us is any more despicable than that which regards the future with complacency, and finds nothing but imperfection in that innocent, creative, and wondering past which the antiquaries and geologists have revealed to us.

For my part I desired to step exactly in the footprints of such ancestors. I believed that, as I followed their hesitations at the river-crossings, as I climbed where they had climbed to a shrine whence they also had seen a wide plain, as I suffered the fatigue they suffered, and laboriously chose, as they had chosen, the proper soils for going, something of their much keener life would wake again in the blood I drew from them, and that in a sort I should forget the vileness of my own time, and renew for some few days the better freedom of that vigorous morning when men were already erect, articulate, and worshipping God, but not yet broken by complexity and the long accumulation of evil. It was perhaps a year ago that I determined to follow and piously to recover the whole of that doubtful trail whereby they painfully made their way from one centre of their common life to the sea, which was at once their chief mystery and their only passage to the rest of their race—from Hampshire to the Straits of Dover. Many, I knew, had written about that road; much of it was known, but much also was lost. No one, to my knowledge, had explored it in its entirety.

First, therefore, I read what had been written about this most ancient way, I visited men who were especially learned in geology and in antiquarian knowledge, I took notes from them, and I carefully studied the maps of all sorts that could help me in my business. Then, taking one companion, I set out late in December to recover and map out yard by yard all that could be recovered and mapped out of The Old Road.

No better task could be put before a man, and the way in which I accomplished it my readers shall judge in the essay which follows this introduction, and in the diary of my journey with which the book shall close.

THE THEORY OF THE OLD ROAD

That such and such Causes determined the Track of the Old Road, and that it ran from Winchester to Canterbury

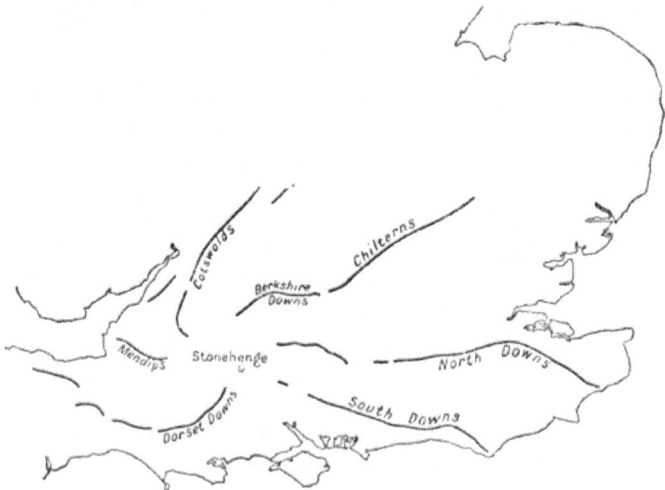

If one looks at a map of England in relief one sees that five great ridges of high land come, the first from just east of north, the second from the north-east, the third and fourth from the east, and the fifth from the south and west, to converge on Wilts and the Hampshire border.

Roughly speaking, their area of convergence is Salisbury Plain, and it has been suggested that Avebury and Stonehenge drew the importance of their sites from this convergence; for these continuous high lands would present the first natural highways by which a primitive people could gather from all parts of the island.

The advantages afforded in the matter of travel by such hills (which are called in great parts of their course the Cotswold, the Chilterns, the North Downs, the South Downs, and the Dorsetshire Downs) are still quite plainly apparent if a man will follow them on foot.

He will see from the heights even to-day the remains of the woodland which made the valleys and the wealds originally far more difficult to traverse. He will note the greater dryness of these heights, and he will remark, if he contrast his cross-country going on the hills with that of the valleys, that the geological formation of these heights, with their contours, fit them peculiarly for an original means of communication.

Four out of the five are great dry, turf-covered ridges of chalk, steep towards the summer sun. The fifth range, the Cotswold, though oolitic and therefore greasy under foot, is at the summit of its western escarpment much drier than the valleys; for that escarpment is steep, and drains off well into the valley of the Severn.

When one has once recognised the importance of these five radiating lines of hills and of their point of convergence, one will next see that of the five, one in particular must have had an especial value perhaps in the very earliest times, and certainly in all the centuries just preceding the historic period, during which Britain, from similarities in religion, language, and blood, was closely connected with the Continent. The passage westward from the Straits of Dover to the Hampshire centres must have been by far the most important line of traffic. We know that it has been so continuously in historic times, and it is easy to prove that long before the opening of our national history with the Roman invasions, some east-to-west road must have been the leading road of England.

Few of the following considerations are new, but all are to the purpose:

. The Straits of Dover are the natural entry into the country. The nature of that entry, and its very great effect upon the development of our island, I will discuss later in connection with the town of Canterbury. How far the Straits may have a rival lower down the Channel I will discuss in connection with the town of Winchester. For the present, the main point is that in the earliest times, whoever came in and out of the country came in and out most easily by the only harbours whence the further shore is visible.

. When the Straits had been crossed and England entered, whither would the principal road lead? The conformation of Kent forced it westward, for the Thames estuary forbade a northern, the only alternative route.

One track of great importance did indeed go north and west, crossing near London. It was later known as the Watling Street; it was the artery which drained the Midlands; it became the connection with sacred Anglesey, ultimately the northern door into Ireland.

But no northern road—whether leading as did the Watling Street to Chester, or bending round as did the Icknield Way north-east after passing the ford of the Thames, or taking the island in diagonal as did the Fosse Way, or leading from London to the Humber as did the Ermine Street, or up at last to the Wall as did the Maiden Way—none of these could have a principal importance until the Romans invented frontiers: frontier garrisons to be fed, and frontier walls to be defended. Before their time this northern portion of England, split by the barren Pennines, hardly cultivated, leading nowhere, could not have been a goal for our principal road. That must have run to the south of Thames, and must have led from the Straits to the districts of which I have spoken—Hampshire, the Mendips, the Wiltshire Hills, Devonshire, and Cornwall.

. The west of the island contained its principal supplies of mineral. Lead indeed was found and exploited in the north, but perhaps not before the Romans, whereas the variety and the amount of the wealth in the valley of the Severn and the peninsula beyond gave all that region an economic preponderance over the rest of the island. Tin, an absolute necessity for the Mediterranean civilisation, was certainly found in Cornwall, though the identification of the Scilly Islands with the Cassiterides is doubtful.

The Mendips formed another metallic centre, presumably richer than even the Devonian peninsula. Lead certainly came in early times regularly from these hills, and Gloucester remained till the Middle Ages associated with the tax on iron.

. There is a fourth aspect of the matter: it is of a sort that history neglects, but it is one the importance of which will be recognised with increasing force if the public knowledge of the past is destined to advance. It is that powers mainly resident in the mind have moulded society and its implements.

That economic tendency upon which our materialists lay so great a stress is equally immaterial (did they but know it) with the laws they profess to ignore, and is but one form of the common power which human need evokes. A man must not only eat, he must eat according to his soul: he must live among his own, he must have this to play with, that to worship, he must rest his eyes upon a suitable landscape, he must separate himself from men discordant to him, and also combat them when occasion serves. The south-west of England has had in this region of ideas from the earliest times a special character and a peculiar value. It is one in spirit with Brittany, with Ireland, and with Wales; nor is it by any means certain that this racial sympathy was the product of the Saxon invasions alone. It is possible that the slower and heavier men were in Kent before Caesar landed, it must be remembered that our theory of 'waves of population' perpetually pressing aborigines westward remains nothing but a theory, while it is certain that the sheltered vales and the high tors would nourish men very different from those of the East Anglian flats or the Weald.

Now one of the forces which helps to produce a road is the necessity of interchange—what physicists call potential—a difference between opposite poles. Such a force is to be discovered in the permanent character of the west; its permanent differentiation from our eastern seaboard. Nor is it fantastic to insist upon the legends which illumine this corner of the island. Glastonbury was for centuries the most sacred spot in our country, and it was sacred precisely because confused memories of an immense antiquity clung round it. The struggle between the Romano-British princes and the heathen pirates, a struggle the main effort of which must have taken place much further east, is yet fixed by legend in that same land of abrupt rocks and isolated valleys which forms the eastern margin of the Bristol Channel, and Arthur, who was king if anything of the Logrians, yet has been given by tradition a castle at Tintagel.

To the west, then, would the main road have gone so far as the mind could drive it.

. The eastern and western road would have been the main artery of southern England, just as the Icknield Way (the north-eastern and south-western one along the Chilterns) would have been the main artery from the Midlands and from the men of the Fens, just as the road along the Cotswold would have been the artery along the Severn valley and from the bend of this at the Wrekin on up into the Fells and the Pennines; and just as that along the Dorsetshire Downs would have been the great means of communication for the Devonian peninsula.

Now of all these districts, the first was by far the most important. Southern and eastern England, Hampshire, Surrey, Sussex, south Berkshire, were the most open and the best cultivated areas, enjoyed the best climate, and were most in touch with the civilisation of the Continent. It is true to say that right down to the industrial revolution the centre of gravity of England lay south of the Thames. In the actual fighting the south always conquered the north, and whereas influence monastic and constitutional would spread from either end of the island, it was the southern which ultimately survived.

There is more. It was along the green-sand ridge of south England that neolithic man had his principal seat. The getting of iron sprang up before history on the red stone of the Sussex weald; it remained there till our grandfathers' time. The oaks that grew from Kent to Devon, along so many creeks from the Rother to the Tamar, built our first ships. They remained our resource for this industry till the Napoleonic wars. The *Victory* was launched in Beaulieu River, and the first eye-witness, Caesar, heard that in cultivation the south had preceded the north.

. Finally, not only was the district the best in England to develop an important road, but the platform or site for that road was ready provided, and invited use much more definitely than did any other way from the narrow seas up into the island.

With this last point I am led to describe the natural causeway which seems to call for a traveller landing in Kent to use it if he would go westward, or for one leaving the inland country to use it as the last part of his journey eastward towards the sea—I mean those heights which are called in their entirety the North Downs.

There runs from the neighbourhood of the Straits of Dover right across south England, in a great bow, a range of hills which for its length, unchanging pattern and aspect, has no exact parallel in Europe.

A man who should leave the Straits with the object of reaching the Hampshire centres would find a moderately steep, dry, chalky slope, always looking full towards the southern sun, bare of trees, cut by but three river valleys (and but one of these of any width), not often indented with combes or projecting spurs: this conspicuous range would lead him by the mere view of it straight on to his destination.

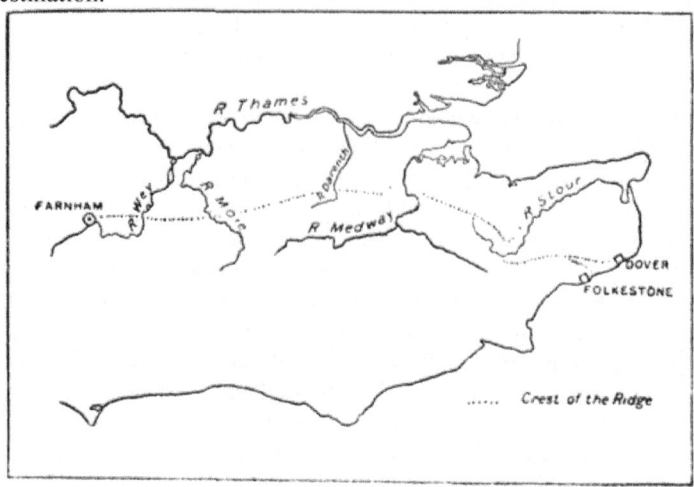

When you have turned the corner of the valley of the Stour, you can see for miles and miles the Kentish Downs like a wall pointing on over the Medway to Wrotham and the villages beyond. When you reach that projecting shoulder of Wrotham Hill you can still see on for miles and miles the straight, clean-cut embankment of chalk inviting you to pursue it westward at such a height as will clear the last cultivation of the valleys, and as will give you some view of your further progress. The end of each day's march is clearly apparent from the beginning of it, and the whole is seen to lie along this astonishingly homogeneous ridge. You do not lose that advantage for perhaps four days of going until you reach the valley of the Wey and the Guildford Gap; and even then for many miles further, though no longer on the chalk but on the sand, a sharp hillside, still looking at the sun, is afforded you in the Hog's Back.

You may say that from the Straits of Dover to Farnham, Nature herself laid down the platform of a perfectly defined ridge, from which a man going west could hardly deviate, even if there were no path to guide him.

THESE PITS WHICH UNCOVER THE CHALK BARE FOR US
See

From Farnham to the converging point near Salisbury, where he would meet the northern, the western, and the south-western roads, no definite ridge continued; but high rolling downs of chalk gave him good enough going, and led him along a water-parting which saved him the crossing of rivers, and afforded for his last two or three days a dry and firm soil.

Such, we must presume, was the full course of the original Road from east to west. To put it the other way round, and give from west to east the primeval track from the centre of south England to the Straits of Dover, we may say that it would leave Stonehenge to enter Hampshire near Quarley Hill, leave Bury Hill Camp on the right, pass near Whitchurch, and so proceeding eastward, following the southern edge of the watershed, would enter Farnham by the line of 'Farnham Lane'; it would thence follow the southern side of the range of hills until it reached the sea above the Portus Lemanis—the inlet which covered the marshy plain below the present village Lympne.

Such was undoubtedly the earliest form of the Old Road, but upon this original trajectory two exceptions fell in a time so remote that it has hardly left a record. The western end of the Road was deflected and came to spring, not from Stonehenge, but from the site of Winchester; the eastern portion was cut short: it terminated, not at some port, but at Canterbury, inland.

Why did Winchester come to absorb the traffic of the west, and to form the depôt and the political centre of southern England? Why did Canterbury, an inland town, become the goal of this long journey towards the narrow seas?

The importance of the one and of the other can be explained. Let me take them in order, and begin first with Canterbury.

The Causes of the Development of Winchester and Canterbury, and of their Position as Termini of the Old Road

The Straits of Dover fill the history of this island because they have afforded our principal gate upon a full life.

All isolated territories—valleys difficult of entry, peninsulas, islands—have this double quality: they are not sufficient to live a full life of themselves, but, receiving sufficient material of civilisation from the larger world outside, they will use it intensively and bring it to the summit of perfection.

Cut off, they wither. Nowhere does humanity fall more abject and lethargic than in such defended places, if the defence be too long maintained. But let them admit from time to time the invasion of armies or ideas, and nowhere does humanity flourish more densely or higher. The arts, the fierce air of patriotism, in whose heat alone the gems of achievement can form, the solution of abstract problems, the expression of the soul in letters—for all these things seclusion provides a special opportunity. It protects their origins from the enemies of seeds, it nurtures their growth with the advantage of a still air, it gives them a resting-place for their maturity.

The valleys prove my thesis. The abandoned valleys of Savoy and Piedmont are goitrous, smitten, sterile. They are the places where, in the Middle Ages, vapid degradations of religion (the Waldensian for instance) could arise; they are the back-waters of Europe. Contrast with them the principal and open valleys; the valley of the Grésivaudan, a trench sown with wealth and vigour, the dale which is the backbone of strong Dauphiné, or that valley of the Romanche from which the Revolution sprang, or that of the Ticino which comes down from the Alps to the Italian plain, rejoicing like a virgin stepping forward into the ample day of her womanhood, arms open and all informed with life. Remember the Limagne and the Nemosian vineyard; I could think that God had made these half-secluded places to prop up our fading memories of Paradise.

And as the valleys, so the islands also prove it. Consider Crete, Cyprus, Sicily—for the matter of that our own island—what they can be when they are linked with neighbouring civilisation, and what when they are cut off.

The place of landing, therefore, is always capital and sacred for islands, and with us that place was chiefly the Kentish shore.

It might seem natural that some special haven upon that shore should absorb our traditions and receive our principal road. It was not so. Canterbury, and no port, received that road and became the nucleus of worship in the island. Why?

Canterbury, and not some port, is the terminus of the Old Road, on account of the effect of the tide in the Straits of Dover. The bastion of Kent, jutting out into the sharpest current of the narrow seas, distorts and confuses the violent tides of the Channel. Now complexity of tides involves a multiplicity of harbours, and many neighbouring harbours among which seamen choose as necessity may drive them, involve a common centre inland.

That is the whole of my argument.

We have already seen how necessarily this corner of England will attract exit and entry. The most powerful emotion connected with that attraction was the sight of land. There is but one small section of the continental coast whence

England, the sun shining on the chalk cliffs, can be clearly seen; and it can be so seen but upon certain days, say one day out of three. The little section lies between Sangatte and Ambleteuse. Here a great hill, whose seaward projection is the cape of Gris Nez, affords a good look-out, and hence I say that at least days out of the year the further shore is visible. On rarer occasions it may be got beyond Calais on the east, and as far as the high sandhills near Etaples on the south and west.

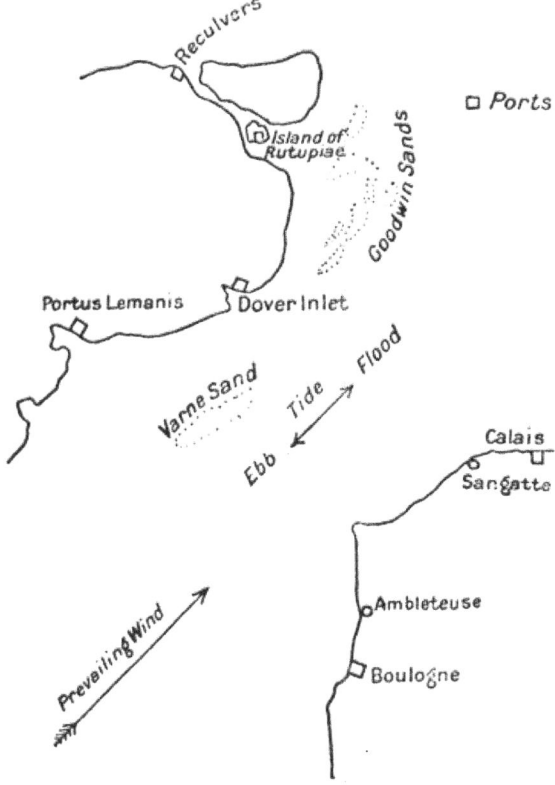

Similarly there is but a small section of the Kentish coast whence the further shore can be seen. It extends from the South Foreland, you may say, to the hill above Folkestone; half a day's walk. There are days when you can see it as far north as Ramsgate Hill, but those days are rare; further west than Folkestone it is hardly ever seen (for the country is flat) save under conditions of mirage, such as startled the people of Hastings at the beginning of the nineteenth century.

There are from the continental side no good starting-points from the coast immediate to Gris Nez; it is rocky, uncertain, and unprovided with inlets. Calais, to the east, was probably the earliest port of departure. Here, at least, is a hole in the land, and there are two considerations which make it probable that the earliest men would start from this side of Gris Nez rather than the other. The first is that they could run as far as possible sheltered from the prevailing winds—for these come from the west and south-west; with such winds they would, up to the point of Gris Nez, be in calm water, while if they started from Boulogne they would have no such advantage. The second is that they could run with an ebb tide down to Gris Nez, and then if the wind failed so that they could not cross in one tide, the flood would be to their advantage when they neared the English coast. It would take them up again under lee of the land, round the South Foreland to Sandwich. From Boulogne they would have to start without shelter, run up on a flood tide, and if they missed that tide they might have drifted down again under the full force of the prevailing wind, any distance along the English coast. Boulogne ultimately became the principal port of exit and entry. It was certainly so used by the Romans; but Calais must, I think, have been the earliest starting-point.

From Calais, then, the run would have been made to the English shores.

But when we note the conditions of this corner of England several things strike us. In the first place, the number of the harbours. These included originally Winchelsea, Rye, the Portus Lemanis, Dover, Richborough, Reculvers; in all six harbours in this small stretch of coast. If we look at the place to-day we find something similar; men will attempt Rye, they will make Folkestone or Dover for choice; Sandwich at a pinch in quite small boats. Ramsgate after Dover gives the best of modern opportunities. There is something more. Most of these harbours were and are bad; most of them were and are artificial.

It is true that in ancient times the strait which divided the Island of Thanet from the mainland afforded an excellent shelter at either end. Reculvers was at one end, and the island of Rutupiae (Richborough) at the other. If one could not get into Richborough and was carried round the North Foreland, one could always beat round into Reculvers; but Dover was not much of a harbour; the Port Lemanis must have been open to the south wind and was probably very shallow; Rye, though better than it is now, was never a steep shore, and was always a difficult place to make. The modern harbours may, without exaggeration, be described as every one of them artificial. Folkestone is distinctly so. The old harbour of Dover has silted up centuries ago, and the gas works of the town are built over its site. Ramsgate would be of no value but for the two constructed piers.

Now what is the meaning of this multiplicity, and of all this interest in preserving such a multiplicity even by artificial means? The tide is the clue to the problem.

Consider a man starting from the continental shore to reach England; consider him sailing with a fresh breeze, for if the breeze was not fresh his chances of crossing in a reasonable time and of making any particular place of landing were small. Consider the fact that if he crossed in a fresh breeze that breeze would be, three times out of four, from the south or west. He runs under the lee of Gris Nez, and when he is beyond that point of rock, he gets into the short, sharp tumble of the sea which is raised by such a wind against the tide, for he has started at the ebb. He runs down with the wind abeam perhaps as far as the end of the Varne (where we now have the Varne Buoy), for the tide so takes him. He sees the water breaking and boiling at this shallow place. It settles near the turn of the tide. He holds on easily, making less westing and pointing well up to the shore. There opens before him a broad but very shallow lagoon with probably some central channel which he knows. He enters and has made the most favourable of the many crossings he knows. It is the Portus Lemanis—our Lympne.

But there are other chances. The wind might fail him, or the wind might so increase that he had to run before it. Did it fail him he would be caught by the flood tide some miles from land. He would drift up along the English shore, getting a few hundred yards nearer with every catspaw, and looking impatiently for some place to which he could steer. The dip in the cliffs at Dover would give him a chance perhaps. If he missed that he would round the South Foreland; he would have the advantage of smooth water, and he would make for the island Rutupiae, which stood at the southern entrance of the strait between the Isle of Thanet and the mainland. If his bad luck preserved, he might be swept up in what we now call the Gull Stream round the North Foreland; but the tide would have been making so long by this time as to be curling round Longnose, and even without the wind he could trust to it almost alone to make Reculvers. Similarly if the wind made him run before it and caused him to miss the Portus Lemanis, he would have the advantage of a weather shore once he was round the South Foreland, and could run with smooth water under him into Rutupiae.

With the prevalent winds, then, and the tidal conditions of the Straits, a multiplicity of harbours was a necessity for this crossing. In a tideless sea—such as the Mediterranean—one harbour, and one alone, would have absorbed the trade of Kent. Under our tidal conditions, a coast most ill-provided was compelled to furnish no less than six.

I could add, were I not afraid of confusing the reader, many other examples of this necessity. For instance, when one runs from the Belgian ports, or Dunkirk, to England, ever so little a change in the wind may make it necessary to go north above the North Foreland. Again, there is the barrier of the Goodwins, which, in spite of legend, is probably prehistoric. If you could not get well south of that barrier at the first trial you had to go north of it. Everything has compelled men, so far, to provide as many chances as possible upon this coast, and at the present day the breakwater at Folkestone, the desperate attempt which many still make to use the harbour of Rye, to some extent the great works of Dover, the poor relic of Sandwich, the continual improvement of Ramsgate, point to the same necessity. Perhaps some refuge less distant from the sea than the estuary of the Swale will be made again to replace Reculvers upon the north of the Kentish coast.

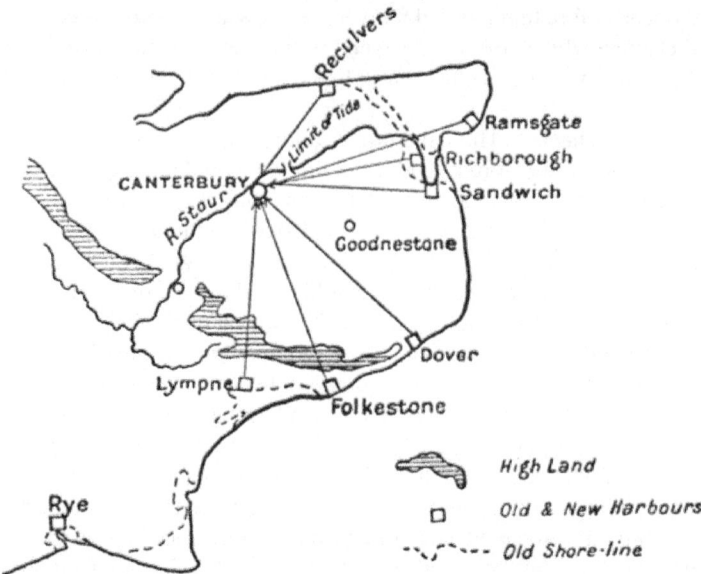

Now it is this multiplicity of Kentish harbours proceeding from the conditions of the tide which has created Canterbury.

When an army has to spread out like the fingers of a hand or the sticks of a fan in order to cover a wide area, it must start from some point of concentration.

When commerce is in doubt as to whether it will use this, that, or another out of many gates, it must equally have this point of concentration.

When defenders are expecting an invasion from many points of a circumference, their only plan is to make their base some central point whence radii depart to that circumference.

When the traveller is uncertain which of six places he can choose for his departure, he will halt at some point more or less central, while his decision is being made for him by the weather or by other circumstances.

When a merchant, landing, knows not in which of six towns he shall land, he must at least be certain that some one town, common as it were to all the six, can be reached the day after his landing; he must know that his correspondents can meet him there, and that he may make that common town his depôt for further transactions inland.

Thus it was that the six Kentish ports and more, standing on the edge of that rounded county, created Canterbury inland.

The town might have stood, theoretically, at any one of a great number of points; geometrically perhaps it ought to have been near the village of Goodnestone, which is the centre of all this circumference from Reculvers round to Lympne. But there is one governing condition which forbids us to look for such a centre anywhere save upon one line, and that condition is the river Stour. It is the only considerable body of fresh water, and the only easy means of communication with the interior. On the Stour, then, would the centre of these ports be.

It might conceivably have been placed as far westward as Wye, for here the Stour traverses the high ridge of land which provides a good road from Dover and Folkestone to the north and west, but though this ridge would have given a reason for the growth of our central town at this spot, there is a better reason for its having risen six miles down stream.

The tendency was to build such a place as near as possible to the tide without losing the advantage of fresh water. In other words, Canterbury represents on a smaller scale the founding of Exeter, of Rouen, and of twenty other towns. Quite a short time ago the tide went up the Stour as far as Fordwych, just below Canterbury, and the presence of the tide up to a point just below the city, coupled with the presence of fresh water flowing from above the city, seems to me to have decided the matter.

The many conjectures upon the primitive state of Canterbury, whether it were a lake village built upon piles, or what not, I do not presume to discuss. The certain matter is that this place was the knot of south-eastern England, and the rallying-point of all the roads from the coast. Caesar landed at Deal, but Canterbury fort was the place he had to take; Augustine landed at Richborough, but Canterbury was the place wherein he fixed the origins of Christianity in England. It was bound to counterpoise that other city of which I shall next speak, and to be for the Straits of Dover what Winchester was for the centre of south English civilisation. It so happened that, of the many characters it might have assumed, the ecclesiastical attached to it. It became the great nucleus of English worship, and the origin, under Rome, of English discipline and unity in the faith for nearly seven hundred years. At last, influencing as much as influenced by the event, the murder of its great Archbishop in the later twelfth century, lent it, for the last three hundred years of its hegemony, a position unique in Europe. Canterbury during those three hundred years was almost a sacred city.

Having said so much, then, about the eastern end of the Road, and why that end was found inland and not upon the sea, let us consider its western region and determine what forces produced the political domination of Winchester.

We have seen that the route from the island centre of Stonehenge and Avebury (the plain where the old roads meet) to the Straits of Dover, may be regarded as the original of our communications across the south of the island, from the rich west to the mainland. Such it might have remained to this day, and such it would certainly have remained throughout the period preceding the Roman invasion, and throughout the barbaric centuries which succeeded the withdrawal of the legions, had not a powerful influence (to repeat what was said above) modified the original track and substituted, at least for its earlier portion as far as Farnham, another road. We know that the great way from west to east which should have had its origin in Salisbury Plain, found it as a fact in Winchester.

Why was this? Why did the encampment or town upon the Itchen gather round itself a special character, and become the depôt into which would stream the lead of the Mendips, the tin of Cornwall, and the armies of all Britain south of Gloucester and west of the Wiltshire Avon? To sum up all these questions we may ask in one phrase, as we asked at Canterbury: What made Winchester?

The answer is again, The Sea: the necessities and the accidents of the crossing of the Channel; and just as Canterbury was made by the peculiarity of the Straits, by the bastion of Kent, confusing and disturbing the rush of the narrow channel, and causing the complexity of meeting tides, so Winchester was made by the peculiar conditions under which the Channel can be passed at what I will call, for the purposes of this essay, the 'Second Crossing': that is, the passage from the jutting promontory of the Cotentin to the southern cape of the Isle of Wight, which stands so boldly out into the sea, and invites adventure from the French shore.

The great opportunity of this passage is far less apparent to us moderns than it was to earlier men. With our artificial methods, especially our regular service of steam, we are ignorant or forgetful of the sea, and the true emotions which it arouses have decayed into the ineptitudes with which we are all familiar. We talk of 'commanding' that element in war; there are even some who write as though we of the towns were native to it; there are very few who understand with what divinity it has prompted, allured, and terrified the past of our race, or under what aspect it may prompt, allure, and terrify the men of a future decline.

By the map alone no one could discover the character of this Second Crossing. After the Straits of Dover the 'sleeve' of the Channel widens so considerably that no clear alternative passage appears to be provided. From Etaples right away to Ushant one might think a sea so wide was of much the same peril and adventure to any early sailor.

Physical experience of many passages corrects such an error; a consideration of the political history of the Continent tends further to correct it. The Second Crossing was, and has always been, and will, we may presume, in the future be, second only in importance to that of the Straits.

□ *Harbours, Modern
and Ancient*

If the narrowing of the sea, due to the northward projection of Normandy and the southern projection of the Isle of Wight, were alone our guide, not very much could be made of it. It is more than double, it is nearly three times the distance between Gris Nez and Shakespeare's Cliff, though far less than the breadth of the Channel either above or below. But the narrowing of the sea at this point is but a small part of its advantage. On either side is the most ample opportunity for protection. On either side high land will comfort and guide a sailor almost throughout the passage, and upon the northern shore is the best conceivable arrangement of chances for his rescue from a gale or from the chance of a tide. The deep estuary of the Seine sufficiently cuts off what is west from what is east of it to make every one upon the western side avoid the difficulty of a journey to Calais and seek some approach of his own to reach England; and south-western England is enough of a unity to demand also a secondary port of its own, whence it may seek the shore of the Continent and escape upon favourable occasions the long journey eastward to the Straits.

Let us consider these points in detail.

The estuary of the Seine was not only an obvious outlet, but it gave an opportunity for the early ships to creep under the protection of a windward shore. From the very heart of the country, from Rouen, and even from Pont de l'Arche, sea-going vessels could go down the stream with a strong tide helping them. They would have calm water as far as the point of Barfleur so long as the wind was south of west, and no danger save the reef of Calvados. Moreover, the trend of the land led them northward in the direction which they knew they had to follow if they were ultimately to find the English coast.

When this defence and indication failed the early sailor, at the corner of the Cotentin, where the land turns west again, he could find the little harbour of Barfleur whence to set out; he was there protected from the outer sea by reefs, and possessed, what was important to him, an excellent shore for beaching. He was sheltered even thus far from the prevailing winds.

Nor was this all. This coast was backed by bold high land, from three hundred feet near the coast to five hundred further inland, and marks of that kind, valuable as they still are, were a necessity to the early navigator. Such land would guide him home if his adventure failed, and it is worth while noticing, in the case of a man to whom all this was a great adventure, the sense of security with which the high hills upon the horizon furnished him in clear weather.

He set out then, and for the first few hours—in theory for close upon twenty-seven miles, and practically for more than twenty of the fifty-three he had to traverse—the French coast was still in sight on such days as could tempt him to cross the sea.

Now, by a happy accident, some of the highest land in the south of England stands dominating the narrowest part of this approach from France. Our Downs in Sussex are commonly receded from the sea-coast; from Brighton westward, their slope up from it is gentle, their escarpment is on the further side, and they are often veiled by the reek of the land. All the way from Beachy Head nothing gives a true mark until you get to this high headland of St. Catherine's Point, which overlooks the narrowest part of the passage.

One must have sailed across here to know how powerful is that hill. It stands steep up out of the sea, it is twice as high as Beachy Head, more than half as high again as Dover Cliff, and though it is but steep turf and not white chalk, it stands up so against the light looking southward, that one may see it at not much less than thirty miles distance as one runs northward so, with the westerly wind just aft of the beam and making for the land. Even in a haze it will stand above the mist and indicate the shore with its head so lifted as to show quite plain in the clearer sky. All this argument will be evident to those who know what a land-fall means. Even to-day, with the compass and the chart, it is the method of all our fishermen in the narrow seas to make some light or foreland, rather than to lay down a course; the violence and the changes of the channel current make it a surer method than any reckoning. In the first days a land-fall was everything. Every memory or relic of primitive navigation shows it a feeling-out for the high, conspicuous blue cloud, which, when you have fixed it once above the horizon, stands permanent and constant, turning at last into no cloud, but an evidence of human things after the emptiness of the sea.

The high land then, of itself, all but bridged the gap. In pure theory one might just catch sight of a fire on the top of St. Catherine's before one had seen the last of a similar flare upon the hills of the Cotentin, and in actual practice, in clear weather, it is but a very short run of fifteen miles or so from the last sight of the French coast to the making of St. Catherine's upon the horizon before one.

These considerations, then, the guide and protection of the Cotentin coast, the inlet of the Seine, the narrowing of the sea, the high land upon either side, would of themselves suffice to point this passage out as a natural way from the Continent to England. Were a man asked to-day where he would rather cross west of Etaples, he would answer, I think, 'from Cherbourg to the Wight'; and very many times, before writing was known or a record kept, men must have run easily through a long summer day, taking it in two tides, losing the land for but a quarter of their voyage, and confident that if evening overtook them, a beacon on St. Catherine's would light the northern horizon, even though half their journey remained to do.

I say this alone would prove the age of the route, but there is something which clinches the argument, and that is what we saw to be so important in the case of Kent—'The Choice of Entry.' How the tides of the narrow seas and the uncertain winds made imperative a choice of entries to the land I have already shown in my discussion of the Straits, and I need not repeat my arguments.

It is enough to remark that in this case of the Second Crossing, conscious human design could hardly have improved the conditions afforded by the Wight.

Behind it is a vast sheltered sheet of water, in shape a tripod, one of the arms of which, five miles in length by nearly one in breadth, is absolutely landlocked and safe in all weathers, while the other two are so commonly smooth and so well provided with refuge at Yarmouth, Lymington, New Town, the Medina, Portsmouth, and the Hamble as to form a kind of large harbour with subsidiary harbours attached.

To this great refuge two entries are provided, each aided by a strong tide, each narrow enough to break the outer sea, but not so narrow as to present grave dangers to small craft.

Supposing a man approaching St. Catherines's Point from the south. The wind fails him, and he is compelled by the tide to drift to the east or to the west; at an equal distance from the point either way he will find an entry into the inland water. Suppose a sudden change in the direction of the wind or in its intensity makes him run before it, from any direction but that of the north (which in itself would provide him with a windward shore) he could make one of the two entries of which I speak. It is true that a nasty shelf and overfalls follow a portion of the shore opposite Ventnor, but, like the reefs of the Cotentin, they do not run so far out as to affect my argument.

There are hardly any conditions under which, after his passage from the Continent, the early sailor would have found it impossible to make either the Needles channel or Spithead. It is a perfect harbour, and though it has but lately recovered its ancient importance, the inland waters, known as the Solent, Southampton Water, and Spithead were certainly, after the Straits, the chief landing-places of these islands. Porchester, Brading, Cowes perhaps, and Bittern certainly, show what the Romans made of the opportunity. All the recorded history of England is full of that group of harbours and that little inland sea, and before history began, to strike the island here was to be nearest to Salisbury Plain and to find the cross-roads of all the British communications close at hand; the tracks to the east, to the west, to the Midlands were all equally accessible.

Finally, it must be noted that the deepest invasion of the land made here is made by the submerged valley of Southampton Water, and the continuation of that valley inward is the valley of the Itchen. The inland town to which the port corresponded (just as we found Canterbury corresponding to the Kentish harbours) is Winchester.

Thus it was that Winchester grew to be the most important place in south England. How early we do not know, but certainly deeper than even tradition or popular song can go it gathered round itself the first functions of leadership. It was possessed of a sanctity which it has not wholly lost. It preserves, from its very decay, a full suggestion of its limitless age. Its trees, its plan, and the accent of the spoken language in its streets are old. It maintains the irregularities and accretions in building which are, as it were, the outer shell of antiquity in a city. Its parallels in Europe can hardly show so complete a conservation. Rheims is a great and wealthy town. The Gaulish shrine of 'the Virgin that should bear a Son' still supports from beneath the ground the high altar of Chartres. The sacred well of a forgotten heathendom still supports with its roof the choir of Winchester.[] But Chartres is alive, the same woman is still worshipped there; the memory of Winchester is held close in a rigidity of frost which keeps intact the very details of the time in which it died. It was yielding to London before the twelfth century closed, and it is still half barbaric, still Norman in its general note. The spires of the true Middle Ages never rose in it. The ogive, though it is present, does not illumine the long low weight of the great church. It is as though the light of the thirteenth century had never shone upon or relieved it.

It belongs to the snow, to winter, and to the bare trees of the cold wherein the rooks still cry 'Cras! cras!' to whatever lingers in the town. So I saw it when I was to begin the journey of which I write in these pages.

To return to the origins. The site of Winchester, I say, before ever our legends arose, had all the characters which kept it vigorous to within seven hundred years of our own time. It was central, it held the key to the only good middle passage the Channel afforded, it was destined to be a capital. From Winchester therefore a road must necessarily have set out to join what had been, even before the rise of Winchester, the old eastern and western road; this old road it would join by a slow approach, and merge with it at last and seek Canterbury as a goal.

The way by which men leaving Winchester would have made for the Straits may have been, at first, a direct path leading northwards towards the point where the old east-and-west road came nearest to that city. For in the transformation of communication it is always so: we see it in our modern railway lines, and in the lanes that lead from new houses to the highways: the first effort is to find the established road, the 'guide,' as soon as possible.

Later attempts were made at a short cut. Perhaps the second attempt was to go somewhat eastward, towards what the Romans called Calleva, and the Roman road from Winchester to Calleva (or Silchester) may have taken for its basis some such British track. But at any rate, the gradual experience of travel ended in the shortest cut that could be found. The tributary road from Winchester went at last well to the east, and did not join the original track till it reached Farnham.

This short cut, feeder, or tributary which ultimately formed the western end of our Road was driven into a channel which attracted it to Farnham almost as clearly as the chalk hills of which I have spoken pointed out the remainder of the way: for two river valleys, that of the Itchen and that of the Wey led straight to that town and to the beginning of the hill-platform.

GLIMPSES OF THE ITCHEN AWAY BEHIND US
See page

It is the universal method of communication between neighbouring centres on either side of a watershed to follow, if they exist, two streams; one leading up to and the other down from the watershed. This method provides food and drink upon the way, it reduces all climbing to the one clamber over the saddle of the ridge, and, if the beginning of the path is struck out by doubtful pioneers, then, as every pioneer in a new country knows, ascending a stream is the best guide to a pass and descending one on the further side is the best guide to open spaces, and to the habitations of men.

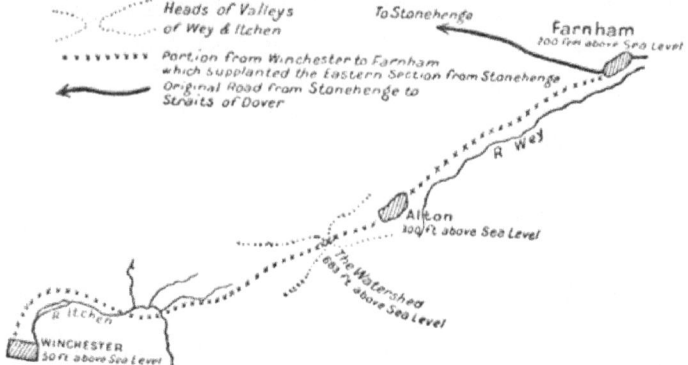

This tributary gradually superseded the western end of the trail, and the Old Road from the west to the east, from the metal mines to the Straits of Dover, had at last Winchester for an origin and Canterbury for a goal. The neglected western end from Farnham to Stonehenge became called 'The Harrow Way,' that is the 'Hoar,' the 'Ancient' way.[] It fell into disuse, and is now hardly to be recognised at all.

The prehistoric road as we know it went then at last in a great flat curve from Winchester to Canterbury, following the simplest opportunities nature afforded. It went eastward, first up the vale of the Itchen to the watershed, then down the vale of the Wey, and shortly after Farnham struck the range of the North Downs, to which it continued to cling as far as the valley of the Stour, where a short addition led it on to Canterbury.

Its general direction, therefore, when it had settled down into its final form, was something of this sort:—

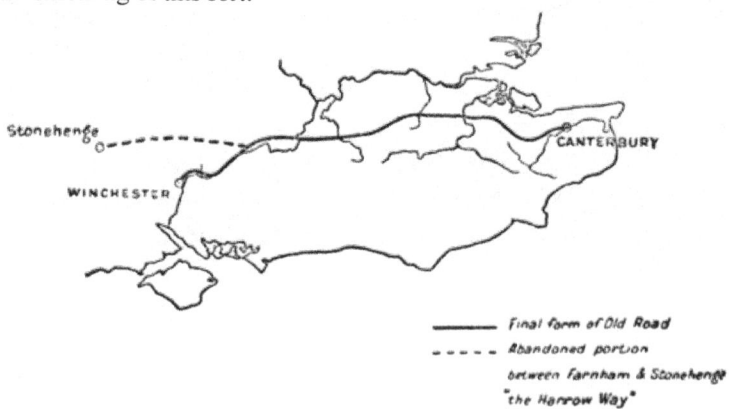

When Winchester began to affirm itself as the necessary centre of south England—that is of open, rich, populated, and cultivated England—the new tributary road would rapidly grow in importance; and finally, the main traffic from the western hills and from much of the sea also, from Spain, from Brittany, and from western Normandy, probably from all southern Ireland, from the Mendips, the south of Wales, and the Cornish peninsula, would be canalised through Winchester. The road from Winchester to Farnham and so to Canterbury would take an increasing traffic, would become the main artery between the west and the Straits of Dover, and would leave the most permanent memorials of its service.

Winchester and Canterbury being thus each formed by the sea, and each by similar conditions in the action of that sea, the parallel between them can be drawn to a considerable length, and will prove of the greatest value when we come to examine the attitude of the Old Road towards the two cities which it connects. The feature that puzzles us in the approach to Canterbury may be explained by a reference to Winchester. An unsolved problem at the Winchester end may be referred for its solution to Canterbury, and the evidence of the two combined will be sufficient to convince us that the characters they possess in common are due to much more than accident.

Of all the sites which might have achieved some special position after the official machinery of Rome with its arbitrary power of choice had disappeared, these two rose pre-eminent at the very entry to the Dark Ages, and retained that dual pre-eminence until the great transition into the light, the Renaissance of civilisation at the end of the twelfth century and the beginning of the thirteenth.

For six or seven hundred years the two towns were the peculiar centres of English life. Winchester was a capital longer than London has been; Canterbury ruled the religion of this island for over nine hundred and forty years.

So much we know for certain, and more may be presumed; but I have conjectured that these sites were of equal importance before the advent of Rome, and such a conjecture needs support. I will maintain that the barbaric centuries which followed the decline of the Empire reproduced in Britain original conditions, and restored their value to sites neglected during the period of Roman order.

Rome, in this frontier province, put her capital in the north, at York, and her principal garrisons in the north also; but even though she did not at first admit their importance, Canterbury and Winchester, with London, insensibly preponderated: London, through which half the roads are marked in the itinerary; Canterbury and Winchester whence, to this day, great Roman roads may be discovered radiating like the spokes of a wheel.

That the importance of these sites should have increased with the increasing barbarism of the Dark Ages is, I repeat, an evidence of their great antiquity. The arbitrary and official forces of society had disappeared. An ancient sanctity beyond history, the track of hunters, the ford, the open hillside, chance opportunities of defence, soil, food, water, all the primal things which determine the settlements of savages, were again at work in the fifth century. The force of merely natural tendencies increased as the consciousness of civilisation faded, and when after the defeat of the pagans in the ninth century Christendom had just been saved and the light slowly began to grow, these forces remained (though with gradually diminishing power) and moulded Europe until the Angevine and the Capetian, the reinvigorated Papacy, the adventure of the Crusades, and the study of the Code, had created once more the fixity of a true civilisation: a civilisation whose institutions and philosophy are our own to-day.

What, then, are the common attributes which we can note in Winchester and Canterbury, which would have drawn savage men to their sites, which therefore give them their tradition, and from which we can induce the causes of their rival power?

Each is near the sea, each near a port or ports; in the case of each, this port, or group of ports, commands one of the two passages to the Continent, and to the homes of civilised men. In each case the distance from the sea is that of a day's march for an army with its baggage. Disembark your men at Southampton or at Dover with the dawn and you hope that night to rest secure behind the walls of Winchester or Canterbury.

The reason of this arrangement was as follows: an inland place has many advantages over a fortified town on the seashore as the resting-place of an army. It has a better food supply; communication from it radiates upon all sides, not only from half its circumference (indeed in many ports there is but one narrow exit along the isthmus of the peninsula or up the valley which forms its harbour). There is likely to be more wood, a matter of great importance for fuel and fortification and sometimes for the construction of engines of war; it will have more fresh water. It may not be a salient, but it is an important, fact that in early times the population of an inland place would be trained for fighting upon land, and its energies would not be divided by the occupation of sea-faring; and finally, your inland fortress is liable to but one form of attack. You may have landed your men after a successful voyage, but, on the other hand, you may have landed them after a hot pursuit. In the first case it is not a disadvantage to sleep the night sheltered by walls inland, and in the second case it is a necessity.

Remembering all these things, it is evident that to have your town of refuge within a day's march of the landing-place is a condition of its value to you. It is far preferable to reach fortification within the daylight than to pass your first halt under the strain of partial and temporary defence.

Winchester and Canterbury are each, of course, upon rivers. They are each upon rivers just above the limit to which the tide would help light-draught, primitive boats, and where yet they could enjoy the fresh water coming down from above. So Caen, so Norwich, and a hundred other cities, have been founded upon rivers a day's march inland from port, and (with the exception of the tide) similar conditions perhaps produced the greatest of all these examples—Rome.

The similarity of the rivers is also remarkable: each of such a size that it can be canalised for traffic above the city, and yet used to turn mills; each supplying industries that depend upon water, especially brewing and tanning; each divided for such a purpose into a number of small regular trenches which flow along the lower streets of the city—an arrangement only possible where a flat site has been chosen—the Itchen, tumbling along the eastern boundary of Winchester, and the Stour, on the northern gate of Canterbury, complete a parallel almost as strong as that of the cities which stand upon them.

They are of much the same length, depth, rapidity of stream, and volume of water. They flow very clear—running over the chalk, clean and potable streams. At a point where each cuts through a range of hills, a point somewhat below the last ancient ford, and just barely above the recorded limit of the tide, a point right on the valley floor where the hills recede somewhat, each bears its city.

Of both towns we are certain that they were prehistoric centres. Not only have the earliest implements of men been discovered in their soil, but it is evident that the prehistoric mode of defence in these islands was used by each—a camp or temporary refuge crowning the hill above the settlement and defended by great circumvallations of earth. Canterbury has the camp in Bigberry Wood; Winchester that upon St. Catherine's Hill. In each town a considerable British population existed before the Roman invasion. In each the coins of British kings struck under the influence of Greek commerce, a century to a century and a half before the Christian era, are to be discovered. The name of each has a British root when it first appears in British history. Canterbury, Durovernum, was the town upon the river bank; and Winchester still preserves the trace of such an origin: the 'Venta' of the Romans: the Celtic 'Gwent'—an open space.

Each was Roman; each occupied much the same area; from each radiated a scheme of Roman roads; upon each the history of Roman Britain is silent; each first appears recorded in the story of the pirate invasions and of the conversion of England after the dissolution of the Imperial scheme.

Such were the two towns which answered each other like peaks over the rich belt of south England. The one the king's town, the other the primate's; the political and the ecclesiastical capitals of all those natural and dark centuries. By a division common to the history of our ancestors in all parts of Europe, one fell naturally to the Court, the other to the Church. The king in Winchester, the primate in Canterbury, 'like two strong oxen pulled the plough of England.' And each, as was necessary to the period, had its great tomb, but not at the same time. Winchester, the capital, had in the Dark Ages its lamp of sanctity. In the Middle Ages this focus moved to the east—to Canterbury. There could be no rivalry. Winchester created its own saint, St. Swithin, with the murder of à Becket Canterbury put out the light of Winchester and carried on the tradition of a shrine; from that time onwards Winchester declines, while Canterbury survives chiefly as the city of St. Thomas.

The Causes of the Preservation of the Old Road; its General Character, and our Application of this in our Method of recovering it

We can regard Winchester, then, and Canterbury, as the point of departure and the termination of the Old Road. We can be certain that it would lie along the upper valleys of the Itchen and the Wey until it struck the Hog's Back, and that thenceforward it would follow the southern slope of the North Downs until these are cut by the river Stour. From that point the last few miles to Canterbury would naturally run parallel with, and in the valley of, the little Kentish river.

But the task which is attempted in this book is more definite than such a general scheme would convey. Many portions of the Old Road have been preserved, many more have been recovered and mapped by the researches of antiquarians; the remaining gaps alone was it our care to explore and settle, until we should, if possible, have reconstituted the whole ancient way, yard for yard, from the capital of Hampshire to the capital of Kent. That was our business, and in order that the reader may follow the more clearly my account of our journey I shall, before beginning that account, set down here, at the end of the present essay, the difficulty which the task presented, how we were aided by certain causes which had conspired to preserve the Old Road, what those causes were, and finally what method we applied to the problem that lay before us.

All archæological research must necessarily repose upon evidence less firm than that of true history, yet a great part of it deals with things lying right to hand.

A barrow is an unmistakable thing. You open it and you find a tomb.

Whatever may be said of paleolithic man, neolithic man has left the most enduring and indubitable evidence. He worked in the most resisting of materials, and he worked well.

A Roman road is a definite thing. Its known dimensions are a guide for our research: the known rules of the Roman engineers. The strata of material, often the embankment, remain. Its long alignments have but to be recovered in a couple of points to establish its direction through a considerable stretch of country. Did a man but know the ridge over Gumber Corner and down Bignor Hill, the Billingshurst Road, the hard foundations through Dorking Churchyard, it would be enough to make him certain of the Stane Street.

But of all the relics of antiquity the prehistoric road is the most difficult to establish.

These old tracks, British, and (if the word has any meaning) pre-British, though they must abound in the island, have become most difficult to reconstitute.

The wild, half-instinctive trail of men who had but just taken on humanity: later a known and common track, but a track still in the hands of savages for countless generations, a road of this kind is preserved by nothing stronger than habit. No mathematical calculation presided at its origin, none can therefore be used to reconstruct it when it has been lost. When (as in the last phase of the road which is the subject of this book) religion may have prolonged its use into historic times, that influence is capable indeed of perpetuating a tradition; but though religion maintains a shrine or a legend it does not add those consistent records of material works which are the best guide for the research of posterity.

The Old Road was not paved; it was not embanked. Wherever the plough has crossed it during the last four hundred years, the mark of it is lost.

From the clay it has often disappeared: from marshy soil, always. On the chalk alone has it preserved an unmistakable outline. Nor can it be doubted that it would have vanished as completely as have so many similar roads upon the Continent and in our own Midlands, had it not been for one general, and three particular, influences which, between them, have preserved a proportion of it sufficient to serve as a basis for the exploration of the remainder.

The general influence was that political sequence by which England has developed a peculiar power for retaining the evidences of her remote past. The three particular influences were, first, the Canterbury pilgrimage; secondly, the establishment of a system of turnpikes in the eighteenth century; thirdly, and most important of all, the chalk.

Consider first the general influence: the effect of English society upon this matter.

This little district of the world is a very museum of such primitive things as lie at the basis of society: of such immaterial things as our existing relics of barbaric polity: of such material things as early systems of defence, the tombs of various forgotten races, the first instruments of iron, bronze and stone; and of my own subject here, the primeval track-ways, in what way has our political history helped to preserve them?

The Empire held this province sufficiently to preserve, but not so thoroughly as to destroy. The districts bounded but untraversed by the great military roads which fed the frontier garrisons must have been left in part autonomous; forbidden indeed to disturb the peace, but not transformed by an ubiquitous administration.

Flourishing as were the very numerous towns, and large as their combined populations must have been, they seem to have remained to the end an archipelago surrounded as it were by a sea of forest and heath, wherein could be found a thin but permanent population, preserving its own language and its tribal system, in touch with the unconquered tribes beyond the Grampians and the Irish Sea, and remaining to the end but half-impressed with the stamp of Latin government.

The picture is but general; exceptions are numerous. Roman estates were cultivated peacefully far from the towns, and certainly nothing dangerous to the ruling man could befall him in the half-conquered tracts of which I speak; but in the rough the picture is true.

Now such a state of things would have among other results this: that it would not destroy the habits of the barbarians, it would crystallise them.

Under such conditions a great activity and wealth accentuated the use of a hundred pre-Roman things. The prosperity which the barbarians enjoyed, the markets in the towns which they must have frequented, would multiply their ancient instruments and would put to a continual use their native trails; and these, as I have pointed out, were not to any great extent overlaid by or forgotten in the new civilisation.

Whatever Gaulish track may have led from Paris to Orleans (and it is historically certain that such a trail did run through the woods to the south of Lutetia), or whatever old track-way was carried along the north of the Apennines, both have wholly disappeared. The great straight causeway of Rome cutting across the Beauce has killed the one, the Æmilian Way the other. So it is throughout nearly all the land which Rome developed, with the exception of this province; here the fragments of a score of British track-ways survive.

When the Empire fell the nature of our decline equally preserved our past. Alone of the Roman provinces the eastern half of Britain was really ruined. It had been exposed for two centuries to the attacks of pirates who came from the unconquered and inexhaustible north. Remote, an Island, impoverished, the first of the frontiers to be abandoned, it was at last overwhelmed: to what extent we can only guess, and in what manner we cannot tell at all, but at any rate with sufficient completeness to make us alone lose the Faith which is the chief bond of civilisation.

The interval was short. There is still some glimmering of light in the middle of the fifth century. In little more than a hundred years communication was reestablished with the Continent, and before the sixth century had closed St. Augustine had landed.

The anarchy had covered a gap no greater than the interval which separates us from the Declaration of Independence, but it had been sufficient to restore to the island the atmosphere of barbarism. There was no Palace, nor any such central authority as everywhere else maintained in the provinces the main traditions of Rome. In the west a medley of Celtic, in the east a confusion of Teutonic dialects had drowned the common medium of thought.

Religion itself when it returned was coloured by the simplicity and folly of the ruin. In the west the unity of Christendom was hardly comprehended, in the east the town of Rome became for the Anglo-Saxons the subject of a sort of idolatry. Letters, geography, common history, glass, and the use of half the metals were forgotten. Not till the Latin re-conquest in the eleventh century was the evil overcome and an organisation at last regained.

But this catastrophe, deplorable as it still remains to history, has proved of the highest value to antiquarians. It produced indeed fantastic legends, stories of the landing of the Horse and the Mare, of Cerdic, Port, Cymric and Wightgar, which have disturbed our national tradition, and which an ignorant bias has credited almost to our own day: alone, therefore, of Western nations have we suffered a real gap in our national story. On the other hand, this gap re-created, as I have pointed out in a former page, those conditions under which the primitive values of hill, wood, marsh, and river reappeared.

The sight of such and such a group of ancient habitations, the meaning to unprotected men of such and such a physical opportunity for defence, in a word, all the influence which topography could exercise on the rudest and most remote of our ancestors, grew real again in the welter and breakdown which we call the Anglo-Saxon period. The artifice and clear creative power of the Mediterranean races was gone: it has never wholly returned to these shores; and what this time chose for the building of cities or the use of roads or of places for defence, is ever an excellent indication of what men had also done long before the Romans came.

How our past has further been preserved by the shape and moulding of the land I shall describe more fully in a further page. There remain to be mentioned two political forces equally conservative. The first is that species of lethargy and contempt which has forbidden us, as it has forbidden every other aristocratic community, to destroy the vestiges of its past. The second is a power more especial but closely allied to this, I mean the influence of the few great owners of the soil.

Whatever results of disorder and of public apathy may proceed from the constitution of this class, and whatever historical learning may have suffered from its power over the universities, prehistoric research has secured from it the greatest advantage, for the landlords of our villages have maintained the antiquities of their manors with the force of a religion. The first barrow to be opened in England was examined by the orders of a great landlord; the fine discoveries of Titsey Park were directly due to the initiative of its owner, the inheritor of Gresham's land. Albury preserves and dignifies one of the critical portions of the Old Road; Eastwell another—and these are but a few of the many that might be cited from this one track-way alone.

We may sum up and say that the political development of England has, in a general fashion, preserved antiquity, and that we owe to it very largely the survival of such relics as the Old Road.

But those particular causes, which have already been mentioned, exercised a more powerful influence: the first of these was the Great Pilgrimage to the shrine of St. Thomas at Canterbury, which arose immediately after his murder in .

To appreciate what that pilgrimage did for the preservation of the Old Road one must grasp the twelfth century.

From just before its opening till a generation after its close, from the final conquests of the Normans to the reign of St. Louis, from the organising plan of Gregory VII. to the domination of Innocent III., from the first doubts of the barbaric schools to the united system of the Summa, from the first troubled raising of the round arch in tiers that attempted the effect of height to the full revelation of Notre Dame—in that years or more moved a process such as even our own time has not seen. It was an upheaval like that by which, in the beginnings of terrestrial life, the huge and dull sea-monsters first took to the keen air of the land. Everything was in the turmoil which the few historians who have seen the vision of this thing have called, some an anarchy, and others a brief interlude of liberty in the politics of Europe. It was neither one nor the other: it was the travail of a birth.

When this young life was once started in the boiling energies of the Crusades:—young Louis VI. the fighter, St. Bernard, the man that would put all into order, young Abelard, who again, after so many silent centuries, began to answer the riddle of the sphinx—when this argosy of youth was launched, the first task of the Church was to attempt to steer it. We know that the Church succeeded, as she succeeded in saving all that could be saved of the Mediterranean civilisation when the Roman Empire bowed, and all that could be saved of our common moral tradition when, after the terrors of the fifteenth century, Europe of the sixteenth threatened to fall into dust.

In the twelfth century the Church captured and rode the new energies, but in that storm of creation a very great deal went down. How much we do not know. It is probable that Rome was still Roman until the Normans sacked it at the beginning of this era. It is certain that the walls surrounding our English cities and those of the northern French and the western Germans were unchanged since the Pagan time, until the expansion of the twelfth century came to break them. I say what relics of primeval learning, what verbal inheritance of primeval experience, were lost in the new violence of Europe, cannot be known. It is enough for us that the essence of civilisation was saved; that if we let go the history of the tribal past with one hand we at least beat off Asia with the other; that if the Romanesque gave up its last spark in that gale, at least the Gothic replaced it.

For the purpose of this book one great loss must be noted: most of the prehistoric roads disappeared.

The unity of Europe, a thing hitherto highly conscious, fully existent, but inactive like the soul of a man in a reverie, sprang into expression and permeated outward things. Men travelled. Inter-communication became within fifty years from a pastime a habit, and from a habit a necessity. Not only the Crusades had done this, but something anterior, some passion for new horizons, which of itself had helped to produce the Crusades. The orders and appeals of a united Church began to circulate throughout Christendom. The universities had arisen, and were visited almost as nomads would visit them: the students crowding now Bologna, now Salerno, now Oxford, and fixing themselves at last, like a swarm of bees, in Paris. The Benedictines had already sketched the idea of the representative system—it was beginning to invade political life. The justice of the central kings went touring on assize. Some say that the cathedral builders themselves were like the soul of Europe wandering from place to place.

With all this the cross-roads developed. Every little village was linked up with every other; the main vague ways, older than history, which joined not even towns directly, but followed only the dry and open of the high lands, necessarily decayed. Some few kept their place. The Watling Street was a necessity; it led from the Straits of Dover to London, and from London to the corner which is the triple gate to Ireland, to Wales and to Strathclyde—the only road by which you can outflank Snowdon if you are going west, the Pennines if you are going west and north. It is still, on the whole, the line of our principal railway. But the Fosse Way began to lose its meaning. The Ermine Street maintained some eminence, for Lincoln was a great town, but the Icknield Way fell into broader and broader gaps. A man would with difficulty discover that the Stane Street was still used.

The road of which this book treats would have disappeared more certainly than any of these.

Winchester was decaying (for England was now quite united, and the north counted in a way), London was becoming more and more—for with intercommunication commerce was arising, and with the harsh efforts of the German against the eastern heathen the Baltic was acquiring a civilisation; with travel the sea was becoming familiar to others than to pirates, and with the sea the port was growing in position—London was becoming more and more, and was already almost the capital of England. Henry II. was perhaps the last king who thought of Winchester as his chief town. London was to overawe his son; his great-grandson was to make Westminster the centre of the constitution.

From Southampton to London the road would remain; the roads from London to Canterbury and to the ports of Kent would grow in importance; but our road, the base of that triangle, would necessarily have decayed: there was less traffic than ever before from west to east, from the Mendips and Cornwall to the Straits. The metals of the Devonian peninsula, and of the Severn valley had lost their economic position, the iron of the Sussex Weald had taken their place. The expeditions to Ireland and the new Scottish problem had removed to Chester and to Lancaster the centres of strategical importance; the same commerce which was giving London its hegemony—I mean the commerce of the Baltic and the North Sea—was developing Orford and King's Lynn, and all East Anglia, and, to a lesser degree, the Humber. The Germanic states had spread so eastward as to draw the life of Gaul also eastward, and to bleed its western promontory; the crossing of the sea between the Cornwalls had lost its old political importance: all combined to kill Winchester, and with Winchester the road from that old capital to Canterbury, when an accident came to preserve that way.

This accident was the murder of Thomas à Becket.

I will not deny that an effect always mingles with its cause; for things that happen are realities, whereas time is not real at all. Not only does the saint make the shrine, but the shrine also the saint. A saint must have come to Canterbury. A primeval site will sooner or later bring to fruit a primeval sacredness. But a study of this kind cannot lose itself in such mysteries. It must confine itself to definite history. In that moment, when the spiritual vision of Europe was at its keenest, when stone itself was to be moulded like clay by the intense vision of things beyond the world, when Suger had conceived the pointed arch at St. Denis, and the gem upon St. Michael's Hill was being cut into its facets, when the Church was most determined to fashion the new world, and to give it a philosophy, and when that task was at its most difficult, from the necessary quarrel between the Soul and the State: that is, between things eternal, personal, inward, and things civic, communal—when the world was fully engaged in such a tangle outward, and the nerves of men, citizens and Christians, were wrought as are those of antagonists in a wrestling match, there fell this blow. For the first time in all these centuries (and at what a time) violence, our modern method, attempted to cut the knot. At once, and as it always must, fool violence produced the opposite of what it had desired. All the West suddenly began to stream to Canterbury, and à Becket's tomb became, after Rome, the chief shrine of Christendom.

Ireland of the saints, South Wales still tribal, still in a way unfixed, lending its population to far adventures and to the attraction of distant places, all the south-western peninsula of England, Brittany for ever mystic, the mountain masses of the Asturias which had themselves preserved an original sanctity, the western ports from Vigo to recently conquered Lisbon—the only ports by which the Christian enthusiasm of the Spaniards conquering Islam could take to the newly opened sea and to the north—all these sent their hordes to converge on Winchester, and thence to find their way to Canterbury.

The whole year came at last to see the passing and re-passing of such men. It was on the th of December that St. Thomas had been struck down. For fifty years his feast had been kept upon that day, and for fifty years the damp English winter had grudged its uneasy soil to the pilgrims: the same weather in which we ourselves traversed it during the journey of exploration which is the subject of this work.

With the jubilee the body was translated in the flush of early summer, and the date of this translation (the th of July) became the new and more convenient day upon which Canterbury was most sought. But the habit of such a journey had now grown so general that every season saw some example of it. The spring, as we know from Chaucer, the winter as we know from the traditional dates preserved upon the Continent, the summer as we know from the date of the chief gatherings: and there must have been a constant return past the stubble and the new plough of the autumn.

It was not only the directness of the Old Road between Winchester and Canterbury that reconstituted its use for the purpose of these pilgrimages: it was also that peculiar association of antiquity and of religion which mingles the two ideas almost into one thing.

The pilgrim set out from Winchester: 'You must pass by that well,' he heard, 'it is sacred.' ... 'You must, of ritual, climb that isolated hill which you see against the sky. The spirits haunted it and were banished by the faith, and they say that martyrs died there.' ... 'It is at the peril of the pilgrimage that you neglect this stone, whose virtue saved our fathers in the great battle.' ... 'The church you will next see upon your way is entered from the southern porch sunward by all truly devout men; such has been the custom here since custom began.'

From step to step the pilgrims were compelled to take the oldest of paths. The same force of antique usage and affection which, in a past beyond all record, had lent their meaning to rocks and springs upon a public way, re-flourished; and once again, to the great pleasure of myself who write of it now, and of all my readers who love to see tradition destroying calculated things, the momentum of generations overcame.

The pilgrimage saved the road. But once started it developed new sanctities of its own, as a tree transplanted will strike roots and take a bend this way or that different from the exact intention of the gardener. In the main it did nothing but preserve the immemorial sites: the cliff above the river Wey, the lonely peaked hill of St. Martha's that answers it from beyond the stream, the cross-roads on the crest of the Downs above Reigate, the ford of the Medway, the entry into the valley of the Stour, it transformed and fixed as Christian things. Our remote ancestry was baptized again, and that good habit of the faith, whereby it refuses to break with any chain of human development, marked and retained for history the oldest things. Upon that rock St. Catherine's was built, upon that hill the Martyrs' Chapel; twin churches in line pointed to the ford of the Medway, the old and dim great battle of the valley was dominated not only by the rude monuments of those who had fallen in it, but by the abbey of Boxley. Charing worshipped the block on which the Baptist had suffered, and the church of Chilham rose on the flank of the hills which had first disputed the invasion of the Romans. What Canterbury became we know.

But this influence, though it was in the main highly conservative, may here and there mislead us.

The new civilisation was well settled before the pilgrimage began. The Normans had governed and ordered for a century; the new taxes, the new system of justice, the new central kingship, had been well founded for over a generation.

The pilgrims, therefore, at certain places did not need to follow step by step the ancient way. They sometimes fail to find us the prehistoric ford, for many bridges and ferries would exist in their time. They sometimes bend right out of the original path to visit some notable shrine, and there is more than one point where another stream of their fellows, coming from London or from the Channel, joins and tends to confuse the track. The occasions are but rare,[] and they are noted here only to explain certain conclusions which will follow in the second part of this book. Taking the pilgrimage as a whole it was the chief factor in the preservation of the Old Road.

Second in the causes of the survival of the Old Road came the turnpikes. The system of turnpike roads served to perpetuate, and in many cases to revive, the use of the old way when the pilgrimage itself was but very vaguely remembered. The tolls chargeable upon these new and firm roads furnished a very powerful motive for drovers and pack-riders to use an alternative route where such charges would not fall upon them. A similar cause was in operation to preserve 'the Welsh road' in the Midlands, and on this southern way of ours there are places when it was in operation, not indeed within living memory, but within the memory of the parents of those now living.

For instance, the road along the summit of the Hog's Back was a better road than the old track which follows the -feet contour upon the south side of the hill; but the summit road was a turnpike for many years during which the lower ill-kept lane was free, and hence a track which, since the Reformation, had served only to link up the little villages of Seale and Puttenham was used once more as a thoroughfare between Guildford and Farnham. A new stream had been diverted into the old channel, and this habit of avoiding the turnpike continued till a date so close to our own time as easily to bridge a gap which, but for that diversion, might have proved impassable. It is not without irony that a system whose whole object was to replace by new and more excellent roads the old rough tracks, proved, indirectly, one of the principal sources of their survival.

The chalk, the third cause of that survival, is of such importance, and that importance is so commonly neglected, that it almost merits an essay of its own.

Consider the various characters which make of this soil the best conceivable medium for the preservation of an ancient road.

Like the sandy heaths and rocky uplands through which other primitive trails would naturally lead, it never paid to cultivate and therefore invited the wayfarer who was not permitted to trespass upon tilled land. But unlike other waste soil, it was admirably adapted to retain the trace of his passage. Long usage will wear into chalk a deep impression which marshy land will not retain, and which hard rocky land will never suffer. Compare, for example, the results of continuous travel along certain of the Yorkshire moors with that which will be produced along the Chilterns above the Thames valley. In the first case very marshy land, perpetually changing, alternates with hard rock. Unless some considerable labour were expended, as in the making of a causeway, neither of these would retain any record of the road when once it had fallen into desuetude. But on the chalk some trace would rapidly form, and with every succeeding year would grow more obvious.

Chalk is viscous and spongy when it is wet. It is never so marshy as to lose all impression made upon it. It is never so hard as to resist the wearing down of feet and of vehicles. Moreover, those who are acquainted with chalk countries must have noticed how a road is not only naturally cut into the soil by usage, but forms of itself a kind of embankment upon a hillside from the plastic nature of the soil. The platform of the road is pressed outward, and kneaded, so to speak, into an outer escarpment, which would make such a track, for generations after it was abandoned, quite plain along the hillside. Finally, there are, or were until lately, no forces at work to destroy such a record. The chalk was little built upon; it had no occasion to be largely traversed by modern roads; it stood up in steep hills whereon no one would have dreamt of building, until the torture of our modern cities drove men to contrast.

How these hills invited, and almost compelled, the primitive traveller to use them has been already described. Once he began to use their soil, better than any other soil in England, it would retain his memory.

Now since some considerable portion of the Old Road has been preserved, a basis for knowledge is afforded. Patches aggregating in length to just over eighty miles are certain and fixed. It is possible to work from that known thing to the unknown, and the gaps where the Road is lost can be recovered by the consistent pursuit of a certain method; this method when it is described will be seen to lend to a first vague and tentative examination a greater value than it seemed to promise. It permitted us to establish by converging lines of proof so much of what had been lost, that one may now fairly call the full course of the Road established from the north gate of Winchester, whence it originates, to the west gate of Canterbury, which is its goal.

A description of our method is a necessary preliminary to that of the journey upon which it was put to the test.

The reconstitution of such a road is essentially the filling up of gaps. The task would be impossible if a very large proportion did not remain evident to the eye, or recorded by continuous history. The task would be much more difficult if the gaps in question were of very great length, succeeded by equally long unbroken pieces of the existing road. Luckily, the record or preservation of the Pilgrim's Way has not fallen upon these lines. There is no continuous gap throughout the whole of these miles of greater length than seven miles, and we have in what may be called the 'known portions,' stretches of ten, thirteen, and even fifteen miles, almost unbroken.

Moreover, the proportion of the known to the unknown is considerable: per cent. of the total distance of miles is known to per cent. unknown, and it must be understood that throughout this book I speak of those parts as 'known' or 'recognised,' which have been universally admitted since the study of the subject was approached by archæologists.

These two facts, the considerable proportion of the known to the unknown, and the absence of any very long stretch in which the Road is lost, facilitate the task in a manner that can be put best graphically by some such little sketch as the preceding, where the dark line is the known portion of the Road. It is evident that the filling up of the gaps is indicated by the general tendency of the rest.

There is a mass of other indications besides the mere direction to guide one in one's research; and a congeries of these together make up what I have called the method by which we approached the problem.

That method was to collate all the characteristics which could be discovered in the known portions of the Road, and to apply these to the search for traces of the lost portion.

Supporting such a method there are the *a priori* arguments drawn from geographical and geological conditions.

There are place-names which point out, though only faintly, the history of a village site.

There is the analogy of trails as they exist in savage countries at the present day.

There is the analogy of other portions of prehistoric tracks which still exist in Britain.

All these confirm or weaken a conclusion, but still the most important arguments are found in the characteristics which can be discovered in the known portions of the Road, and which may be presumed, in the absence of contradictory evidence, to attach to the lost portions also.

When a gap was reached, it was necessary to form an hypothesis to guide one in one's next step, and such an hypothesis could best be formed upon a comparison of all these various kinds of knowledge. The indication afforded by any one of them would, as a rule, be slight, but the convergence of a number of such indications would commonly convey a very strong presumption in favour of some particular track.

It was then our business to seek for some remaining evidences, apparent to the eye, whereby the track could be recovered. Such evidences were the well-known fact that a line of very old yews will often mark such a road where it lies upon the chalk; the alignment of some short path with a known portion behind, and a known portion before one; while, of course, the presence of a ridge or platform upon such an alignment we regarded (in the absence of any other lane) as the best guide for our search.

Occasionally, the method by which we brought our conjecture to the test had to be applied to another kind of difficulty, and a choice had to be made between two alternative tracks, each clear and each with something in its favour; in one or two short and rare examples, the Road very plainly went one way, when by every analogy and experience of its general course it should have gone another. But, take the problem as a whole, whether applied to the commonest example, that of forming an hypothesis and then finding whether it could be sustained, or to the most exceptional (as where we found the Road making straight for a point in a river where there was no ford), the general method was always the same: to consider the geographical and geological conditions, the analogy of existing trails of the same sort, the characters we had found in the Road itself throughout its length as our research advanced, and to apply these to the parts where we were in doubt.

The number of 'habits,' if I may so call them, which the Road betrayed, was much larger than would at first have appeared probable, and that we could discover them was in the main the cause of our success, as the reader will see when I come to the relation of the various steps by which we reconstituted, as I hope, the whole of the trail.

The principal characteristics or 'habits' are as follows:—

I. The Road never turns a sharp corner save under such necessity as is presented by a precipitous rock or a sudden bend in a river.

In this it does precisely what all savage trails do to-day, in the absence of cultivated land. When you have a vague open space to walk through at your choice you have no reason for not going straight on.

We found but one apparent exception to this rule in the whole distance: that at the entry to Puttenham; and this exception is due to a recent piece of cultivation.[] This alignment, however, is not rigid—nothing primitive ever is—the Road was never an absolutely straight line, as a Roman road will be, but it was always direct.

II. The Road always keeps to the southern slope, where it clings to the hills, and to the northern bank (*i.e.* the southward slope) of a stream. The reason of this is obvious; the slope which looks south is dry.

There are but four exceptions to this rule between Winchester and Canterbury, and none of the four are so much as a mile in length.[]

III. The road does not climb higher than it needs to.

It is important to insist upon this point, because there is nothing commoner than the statement that our prehistoric roads commonly follow the very tops of the hills. The reason usually given for this statement is, that the tops of the hills were the safest places. One could not be ambushed or rushed from above. But the condition of fear is not the only state of mind in which men live, nor does military necessity, when it arises, force a laden caravan to the labour of reaching and following a high crest. The difficulty can be met by a flanking party following the top of the ridge whose lower slope is the platform for the regular road. In this way the advantage of security is combined with the equally obvious advantage of not taking more trouble than you are compelled to take. There are several excellent examples of the flanking road on this way to Canterbury, notably the ridge-way along the Hog's Back,[] which has become the modern high-road; but nowhere does the Old Road itself climb to the top of a hill save when it has one of two very obvious reasons: (*a*) the avoidance of a slope too steep to bear the traveller with comfort, or (*b*) the avoidance of the ins and outs presented by a number of projecting ridges. On this account at Colley Hill, before Reigate, and later, above Bletchingly, near Redhill, the Road does climb to the crest: and so it does beyond Boughton Aluph to avoid a very steep ravine. Once on the crest, it will remain there sometimes for a mile or so, especially if by so doing it can take advantage of a descending spur later on: as after Godmersham Park down to Chilham. But, take the Road as a whole, its habit when a convenient southerly bank of hills is present, is to go up some part of the slope only, and there to run along from to feet above the floor of the valley. If it be asked why the earlier traveller should have been at the pains of rising even so much as this, it may be noted that the reason was threefold: it gave the advantage of a view showing what was before one; it put one on the better drained slope where the land would be drier; and it lifted one above the margin of cultivation in later times when men had learned to plough the land. In the particular case of this Road it had the further advantage that it usually put one on the porous chalk and avoided the difficult clay of the lower levels.

IV. Wherever the Road goes right up to the site of a church it passes upon the southern side of that site.

It is necessary to digress here for a moment upon the archæological importance of these sites. They are but an indication, not a proof, of prehistoric sanctity. It would be impossible to say in what proportion the old churches of these islands stand upon spots of immemorial reverence, but it is certain that a sufficient proportion of them do so stand (the church of Bishopstoke, for instance, upon the site of a Druidical circle), as to afford, when a considerable number are in question, a fair presumption that many of the sites have maintained their meaning from an age long prior to Christianity. Apart from the mass of positive evidence upon this matter, we have our general knowledge upon the methods by which the Faith supplemented, and in part supplanted, older and worse rituals; and there is an impression, which no one who has travelled widely in western Europe will deny, that the church of a place has commonly something about it of the central, the unique, or the isolated in position; characters which cannot wholly be accounted for by the subsequent growth of the community around them.

Now, on its way from Winchester to Canterbury, the Old Road passes, not in the mere proximity of, but right up against, thirteen existing or ruined churches. They are, proceeding from west to east, as follows: King's Worthy, Itchen Stoke,

Bishop Sutton, Seale, Puttenham, St. Martha's, Shere, Merstham, Titsey, Snodland, Burham, Boughton Aluph, and Chilham. In the case of eight it passes right up against the south porch; in the case of two (Bishop Sutton and Seale) it is compelled to miss them by a few yards. One (St. Martha's) is passed on both sides by a reduplication of the track. One (Chilham) is conjectural, and the last (Shere) is doubtful.

THE CHURCH OF SHERE

The habit is the more remarkable from the fact that the Road commonly goes north of a village, and therefore should, unless it had some purpose, commonly go north of all churches. And, indeed, it does pass many churches to the north, but it always leaves them (as at Chevening, Lenham, Charing, and the rest) to one side. It never goes close to their site.

The importance of this rule will be apparent when we consider, later on, the spots in which a church stands, or has stood, and where, at the same time, the track is doubtful and has to be determined.

V. In crossing a river-valley, the Road makes invariably for the point where spurs of dry ground and rising ground come closest upon either side, and leave the narrowest gap of marshy land between.

I note this as a characteristic of the Road, quite apart from the more obvious considerations; such as, that primitive man would seek a ford; that he would seek gravel rather than clay; that he would try to pass as high up a river as possible, and that, other things being equal, he would keep to the general alignment of his path as much as possible in crossing a river. All these are self-evident without the test of experience, but this characteristic of which I speak is one that would not occur to a traveller who had not tested it with his own experience. It is so at the crossing of the Itchen, at the crossing of the Wey, at the crossing of the Mole, at the crossing of the Darent, and, as we shall see, it is useful in giving us a clue towards the much more important crossing of the Medway.

VI. Where a hill must be taken, it is taken straight and by the shortest road to the summit, unless that road be too steep for good going.

Here one has something to be found all over England where an old, has been superseded by a modern, way. I have an instance in my mind on the main road westward from Tavistock into Cornwall. It is exactly analogous to what the Indian trails in America do to the present day. It is civilisation or increased opportunities—especially the use of wheeled traffic on a large scale—which leads men to curve round a hill or to zig-zag up it. In the course of the Old Road there are not many examples of this. From the nature of the ground which it traverses the hills to be surmounted are few; but when they do come, the knowledge of this habit will lead one always to prefer the straightest of two ways of reaching the summit.

VII. A similar tendency causes the Road to seek, as immediately as possible, when it is passing from one valley to another, the saddle of the watershed, if that watershed be high.

Of this there is but one example in the Old Road, that near Medstead in Hampshire. It therefore affords us no particular clue in dealing with this road alone, but as we know that the same phenomenon is apparent in the remaining prehistoric tracks, and in existing trails in savage countries throughout the world, it is a valuable clue, as will be seen later in the particular instance of the saddle between the valleys of the Itchen and the Wey.

Prepared for such a method; having well marked our maps and read what there was to read; having made certain that the exact starting-point was the site of the North Gate at Winchester, and that the first miles went along the right bank of the Itchen, we two went down from town before December ended, choosing our day to correspond exactly with the dates of the first pilgrimage. When noon was long past, we set out from Winchester without any pack or burden to explore the hundred and twenty miles before us, not knowing what we might find, and very eager.

THE EXPLORATION OF THE ROAD
THE EXPLORATION OF THE ROAD
Winchester to Alton
Eighteen miles and a half
Winchester differs from most other towns which the Romans reorganised in that its main streets, the street north and south and the street east and west, do

The Old Road

not divide the city into four equal quarters. The point where the two ways cross is close to the western wall, and this peculiar arrangement was probably made by the first conquerors in order to avoid an exit upon the marshy land beside the Itchen; for that river flowed just against the eastern wall of the city.

Of the four arms of this cross, the northern, a street always given up to commerce, became, in the later Middle Ages, the Jewry. By a process at first perhaps voluntary, but later legal, the Jews were concentrated into one quarter, a sort of Ghetto. It is to be noticed that in nearly every case these Jewish quarters were in the very thick of a city's life, and (as in the Paris of Philippe le Bel) of far greater value than any other equal area of the city.[] Something of the kind was present at Winchester. The whole stream of traffic which passed out from the capital to the rest of England went through the lane of the moneylenders, and we may say with certitude that the north gate, the limit of that lane, was the starting-point of the Old Road.

The north gate has now disappeared. It lay just south of the grounds now known as North-Gate House. The deflection of the street is comparatively modern; the original exit was undoubtedly (as at Chichester and elsewhere) along the straight line of the Roman road. This passed near the site of the present house, and pointed towards the isolated tree which marks the northern edge of the garden.

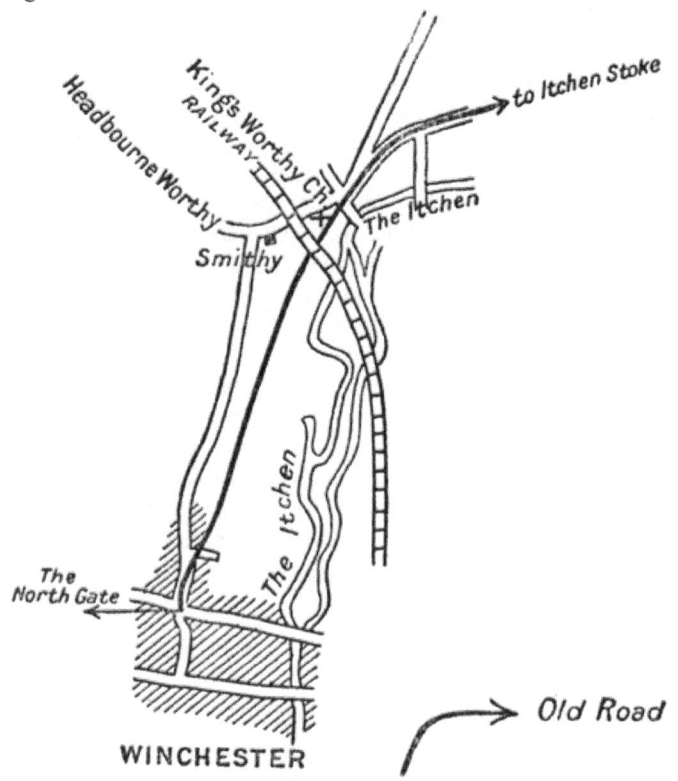

From this point it has been commonly imagined that the Old Road must have coincided with the modern Hyde Street, and have followed this line as far as the smithy at Headbourne Worthy. Thence it has been supposed to branch off to King's Worthy.

From the church of that village onwards through Martyrs' Worthy and Itchen Abbas no one questions but that the modern highway is identical with the Old Road; but I think the original track may be shown to have proceeded not along the modern street, but by an interior curve, following up the Monks' Walk, passing under the modern railway embankment near the arch which is just north of the Itchen bridge, and making thence straight for King's Worthy church, thus leaving Headbourne Worthy on the left, and running as the thick line runs in this sketch-map.

The point evidently demands argument, and I will give the arguments upon one side and upon the other, so that the conclusion may recommend itself to my readers.

In favour of the first supposition there is this to be said, that the line through Headbourne Worthy carries the road all the way above the levels which may be marshy, avoids the crossing of any stream, and indicates in the continuity of the place-names (the three Worthies)[] a string of similar sites dating from a similar antiquity. To this consideration may be added that parallel between Canterbury and Winchester which will be found throughout this essay. For at the other end of the road the entry into Canterbury is of a similar kind. The Old Road falls, as we shall see, into Watling Street, a mile before the city, and enters the ecclesiastical capital by a sharp corner, comparable to the sharp corner at Headbourne Worthy in the exit from Winchester.

Against all this one can array the following arguments. The Old Road, as the reader has already seen, never during its course turns a sharp corner. It has to do so at Canterbury because it has been following a course upon the north bank of the Stour, the bank opposite from that upon which Canterbury grew; no better opportunity could be afforded for crossing the river than the ferry or bridge which the most primitive of men would have provided as an entry into their township, and such a bridge or ferry would necessarily run at right angles to a path upon the opposite bank.

No such necessity exists in this case of the exit from Winchester. The town is on the same bank of the river as the road. Had the Old Road left by the eastern gate, such a corner would have been quite explicable and even necessary, but as a matter of fact it left by the northern.

The argument which relies upon the necessity of following the high land is of more value; but that value may be exaggerated. The shorter and more natural track, to which we inclined, though it runs indeed at a lower level, follows the edge of the chalk, and just avoids the marshy alluvial soil of the valley.

The objection that it compels a crossing of the little stream, the Bourne, is not so well founded as might be imagined. That stream would indeed have to be crossed, but it would have been crossed under primitive conditions in a much easier fashion than under modern. Its depth and regularity at the present day are the result of artifice, it runs at an unnatural level embanked in a straight line along the Monks' Walk, and was perhaps turned, as was nearly every stream that served a medieval congregation, for the purpose of giving power to the mill of the Hyde Abbey and of supplying that community with water.

The mention of the stream and of the monastery leads me to two further considerations in support of the same thesis. This splendid monument of the early twelfth century and of the new civilisation, the burial-place of the greatest of our early kings, the shrine which stood to royal Winchester as St. Germain des Prés did to royal Paris, and Westminster later to royal London, would, presumably, have had its gates upon the oldest highway of its time.

It should be remarked also that before its deflection that brook must have followed the slope and fallen into the Itchen by a much shorter and smaller channel, reaching the river near where the railway bridge now stands. A portion of its water still attempts a similar outlet, and there can be little doubt that before the embankment of eight hundred years ago the fields we traversed in our search for the path would have been dry, for they are high enough to escape flood, and they have a sufficient slope, and their chalky soil is sufficiently porous to have left the land firm upon either side of the little stream.

The Roman road also took the same line, at least as far as King's Worthy; and a Roman road was often based upon a pre-Roman track.[]

The path so taken not only turns no abrupt corner (in itself an excellent argument in support of its antiquity), but points directly to King's Worthy church so as to pass its *south* porch, and then curves easily into that modern highway which goes on to Martyrs' Worthy and Itchen Stoke, and is admittedly coincident with the Old Road.

The alternative has no such regular development; if one comes through Headbourne Worthy one is compelled to turn a sharp corner at the smithy of that village and another just upon King's Worthy church before one can fall in with the modern road at the point where its coincidence with the old one ceases to be doubtful.

From all these considerations we determined to follow the lower and more neglected path as representing the track of the Old Road.

We left Hyde Street by the first opening in the houses of its eastern side; we halted with regret at the stable door, still carved and of stone, which is the last relic of Hyde Abbey. We saw the little red-brick villas, new built and building, that guard the grave where Alfred lay in majesty for six hundred years.[]

We went up the Monks' Walk, under the arch, past King's Worthy church, through King's Worthy village and so on through Martyrs' Worthy to Itchen Abbas. It is a stretch which needs little comment, for after King's Worthy the modern high-road certainly corresponds with the ancient track. We were walking these few miles upon earth beaten (to quote recorded history alone) by the flight of Saxons from the battle of Alton, and by the conquering march of Swegen which was the preliminary to the rule of the Danes over England. We noted the sharp dip down into the valley[] (whence Itchen-A-Bas is thought to take its name), and on reaching the green at Itchen Stoke, six miles from our starting-point, we determined to explore the first considerable difficulty which the road would present to us.

That difficulty we had already presupposed to exist from a study of the map before we undertook our journey, and an examination of the valley confirmed us in our conjecture.

Thus far the history of the Worthies, and, as we have seen, the topographical necessities of the valley had determined the way with some accuracy; the most of it had corresponded to the present high-road. At Itchen Stoke these conditions disappeared.

The valley of the Itchen here makes a sharp bend northwards round a low but rather difficult hill, and leads on to the Alresfords. The modern road follows that valley, passes through New Alresford, and there joins the main road from Winchester to London.

The Old Road did not follow this course. It crossed the river at Itchen Stoke, crested the hill, and did not join the London road until the point marked by the church at Bishop Sutton, one mile from Alresford. That its track was of this nature can be proved.

We had already noted, upon the earlier maps, that, barely a century ago, nothing but irregular lanes connected Itchen Stoke with the Alresfords by the valley of the river. These could not represent the original trail; where that trail passed we were able to discover. The word Stoke here, as elsewhere in the South Country, is associated with the crossing of a stream. It stands for the 'staking' which made firmer the track down through the marshy valley, and supported on either side the wattles and faggots by which an approach to a river was consolidated. Moreover, to this day, a ford exists at Itchen Stoke, and it is an obvious place for passing the river; not only is the water shallow, but the bottom is firm, and the banks are not widely separated, as is so often the case where the depth of a river is lessened.

This ford, by itself, might not mean much. There are plenty of reasons for crossing a stream whenever one can, and Itchen Stoke would have provided a convenient ford for any one living north of the river who desired to get south of it. But there are a number of other considerations, which confirm to a point of certitude the crossing of the river by the Old Road at this point. Just above Itchen Stoke is the confluence of all the head-waters which form the Itchen: the Alre, and other streams. Now a confluence of this kind is invariably marshy, and this marsh could not, in early times, have been avoided (if one followed the flat right bank) save by a very long bend to the north: along that bend no trace of a road or of continuous prehistoric use exists: while, if one crosses at Itchen Stoke to the other bank, one finds a steep, dry bank on which to continue one's journey.

THE HEAD-WATERS WHICH FORM THE ITCHEN, THE ALRE AND OTHER STREAMS

It might be argued that the traveller would have wished to take on his way such settlements as the Alresfords; but though it is true that an ancient track leaves Old Alresford to the north-east, that track does not point to Farnham, the known junction of the 'short-cut' from Winchester with the original 'Harrow Way.' Old Alresford is well to the west, and also too far to the north of the track we had followed to be touched by it save at the expense of an abrupt and inexplicable bend. New Alresford is nearer the alignment (though not on it), and it is to New Alresford that the modern road leads. But the town was not in existence[] till the end of the twelfth century, and only grew up in connection with Bishop Lucy's scheme for rendering the Itchen navigable. The pond which was the head of that undertaking still remains, though much diminished, the chief mark of the place.

The ford might have been used, and is still used, for reaching all the district south of the Itchen, but that district was high, bare, waterless, unpeopled, and of no great importance until one got to the Meon valley, and it is significant that the Meon valley was in its earliest history independently colonised and politically separate from the valley of the Itchen.

In this absence of any but a modern road up the valley to the Alresfords, in the presence of the marsh, in the eccentricity of Old and the modernity of New Alresford, and in the unique purpose attributable to the ford, we had a series of negative considerations which forbade the Old Road to follow the river beyond Itchen Stoke.

On the other hand, there are as many positive arguments in favour of the thesis that the ford was used by the oldest road from Winchester to Farnham.

Between these two centres, as will be seen in a moment by the sketch-map on p. , a high but narrow watershed had to be crossed. To approach this watershed by the easiest route must have been the object of the traveller, and, as the map will show, to cross at this ford, go straight across the hill to Bishop Sutton, and thence follow the Ropley valley was to go in a direct line to one's object.

As we talked to the villagers and gathered their traditions, we found that this ford had been of capital importance. The old church of the village stood just beside the river, and in such a position that the road to the ford passed just by its *southern* porch. It has disappeared—'in the year of the mobbing,' say the peasants: that is, I suppose, in ; but the consecrated land around it is still enclosed, and its site must have clustered the whole place about the riverside. It stood, moreover, close against the ford; and the Old Road that skirted the churchyard is marked by an alignment of yews and other trees leading directly to the river.

Finally, when we accepted the hypothesis and crossed the river, we found a road corresponding to what the old track should be. It has in the past been somewhat neglected, but it is now a metalled lane; it is without any abrupt turn or corner, and leads directly over the hill in the direction of Bishop Sutton, the Ropley valley, and so at last to the watershed, the surmounting of which was the whole object of the trail from this point onwards.

The points I have mentioned will be made clearer, perhaps, by a sketch-map, in which the dark patches and lines represent the water-ways at this confluence which forms the Itchen. The Old Road I have indicated by a dotted line, but for its exact course it would be advisable for readers to refer to an Ordnance map.

All these pieces of evidence supporting one another seemed to us sufficient to determine the trajectory at this point. The ford, the position of the church, the number of streams that would have to be crossed were the valley to be further pursued, the low marshy ground at the confluence of these streams, the non-existence of any ancient settlement or trace of a road at the base of Alresford Hill, the fact that the only village to which such a track could lead is of comparatively recent creation, the existence of an old track, direct in its alignment, proceeding straight from the ford, and pointing without deviation to Bishop Sutton church and the Ropley valley—all these facts combined settled any doubts upon the way we should go. We climbed and followed the lane to the top of the hill.

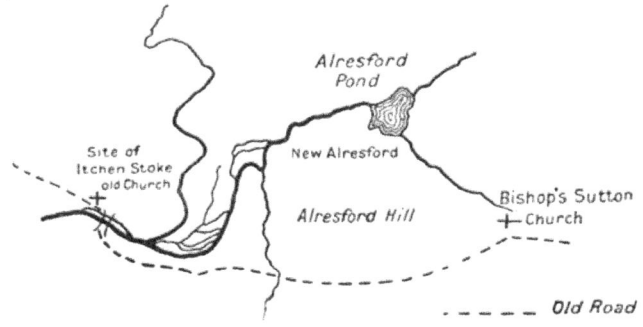

These two miles of the way gave us (under the evening—for it was the falling of the light) glimpses of the Itchen westward and away behind us. The road had the merit of all savage trails, and of all the tracks a man still takes who is a-foot and free and can make by the shortest line for his goal: it enjoyed the hills. It carried two clear summits in its flight, and from each we saw those extended views which to the first men were not only a delight, but a security and a guide. It was easy to understand how from these elevations they planned their direct advance upon the ridge of the watershed which lay far before us, eastward, under the advancing night. As they also must have done, we looked backwards, and traced with our eyes the sharp lines of light in the river we had just abandoned. We so halted and watched till darkness had completely fallen; then we turned down northward to Alresford to sleep, and next morning before daybreak, when we had satisfied the police who had arrested us upon suspicion of I know not what crime, we took the hill again and rejoined the Old Road.

By daylight we had come down Whitehill Lane, the steep pitch into Bishop Sutton, and were tramping up that vale which makes for the watershed, and so leads to the corresponding vale of Alton upon the further side.

Here, at least as far as the Anchor Inn, and somewhat further, the modern highway corresponds to the Old Road. It thus follows the lowest of the valley, but there is no reason at first why it should not do so. The rise is fairly steady, the ground dry (an insignificant stream gradually disappears beneath the chalk), and the direction points straight to the shortest approach for the ridge which cuts off the basin of the Channel from that of the Thames.

This direction, does not, however, long continue. The valley curves somewhat to the north, and it might be presumed that the original way, making more directly for the saddle of the watershed, would gradually climb the southern hillside. By so doing it would find two advantages: it would take a shorter cut, and it would conquer at one stretch, and rapidly, the main part of the feet between the Anchor Inn and the summit.

It was but a guess that the Old Road would probably take a straight line upwards. The curve of the modern road does not carry it more than half a mile from the direct alignment. The Old Road might quite well have suffered such a deviation, and we were in some doubt when we proceeded to gather our evidence. That evidence, however, proved fairly conclusive.

There is a tradition, which Mrs. Adie has justly recognised, that the pilgrims of the Middle Ages passed through Ropley.[] What is more important to our purpose, Ropley has provided a discovery of British antiquities, Celtic torques, near the track which the more direct line to the watershed would presuppose.

We had further the place-name 'Street' to guide us: it is a word almost invariably found in connection with a roadway more or less ancient; later on we found many examples of it upon this same road.[] Here the hamlet of Gilbert Street lay to the south of our hypothetical alignment, and another, named North Street, just to the north of it.

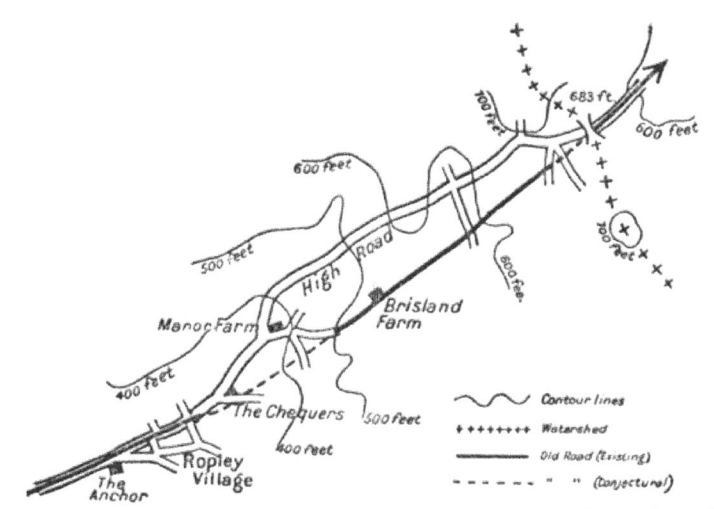

We further noted upon our map that a very considerable portion of the exact alignment drawn from the main road at the Anchor Inn to the saddle of the watershed would coincide precisely with a lane, which, when we came to examine it, gave every evidence of high antiquity.

Possessed of such evidence, it was our business to see whether investigation upon the spot would confirm the conclusion to which they pointed. There was enough discovered so to confirm it, though the Old Road at this point has disappeared in several places under the plough.

The course of our discovery will be best followed with the aid of this rough map, whereon are sketched the contour-lines, the trace of the Old Road, and the watershed.

About half a mile from the 'Anchor' at the end of the avenue of trees which here dignifies the turnpike and just after the cross-roads,[] in a meadow which lay to the right of the road, my companion noticed an embankment, perfectly straight, slightly diverging southward from the main road as the line we were seeking should diverge, and (as we found by standing upon it and taking its direction) pointing directly at the saddle of the watershed. Whether it was continued through the garden of the Chequers Inn (a very few yards) I would not trespass to inquire: in the three fields beyond, it had entirely disappeared.[] After this gap, however, there is a boundary, with an old hedge running along it and a path or cartway of a sort.[] These carry us exactly the same direction down a short slope, across a lane called Cow Lane, and on to the Manor Farm at North Street. During this stretch of a mile there was nothing more to guide us. The division between fields and properties very often follows the line of some common way: one could not say more.

But the significant fact which, as we believe, permitted us to bridge the gap was this: that the embankment we had first discovered, and the hedge and path (which proceeded in the same line after the loss of the road over the two fields) each pointed directly towards the lane (Brisland Lane) which we entered close to the Manor Farm,[] which presented, as we found, such marks of antiquity,

49

which takes the hill steeply, and which, on the plateau above, continues to aim straight at the saddle of the watershed.

It is difficult to express in a written description the sentiment of conviction which the actual view of such an alignment conveyed. When we had followed the lane up the steep hill and stood by Brisland farmhouse, looking back from that height we could see the lane we had been following, the hedge, the corner of the garden of the 'Chequers,' the embankment beyond, all in one, stretched out like parti-coloured sections of one string, and the two gaps did but emphasise the exactitude of the line.

Turning again in the direction which we were to follow, the evidence of ancient usage grew clearer.

We were upon one of those abandoned grassy roads, which are found here and there in all parts of England; it ran clear away before us for a couple of miles.

It was very broad—twenty yards perhaps. The hedges stood upon either side, guarding land that had been no man's land since public protection first secured the rude communications of the country. No one who had seen portions of the Icknield Way upon the Chilterns, or of this same Old Road where it has decayed upon the Kentish hills, could doubt the nature of what we saw. Long fallen into disuse, it had yet escaped the marauding landlords during three centuries of encroachment. They had not even narrowed it. So much of its common character remained: it was treeless, wide, and the most of it neglected; never metalled during all the one hundred and fifty years which have transformed English highways. It was the most desolate, as it was the most convincing, fragment of the Old Road we had set out to find.

It had an abominable surface; we had to pick our way from one dry place to another over the enormous ruts which recent carts had made. For generations the lane had been untenanted; but there is a place where, in the last few years, an extraordinary little town of bungalows and wooden cottages had arisen upon either side of the lane.

Not satisfied with the map, we asked of a man who was carrying milk what local name was given to this venerable street. He told us that the part in which we were walking was called Blackberry Lane, but that it had various names at different parts: and as he could tell us nothing more, we left him.

At the very summit this way joined a modern, well-made lane, called Farringdon Lane, turned to the left and north, and immediately fell into the main London road, which had been climbing from the valley below and was here at the thirteenth milestone. The Old Road, suffering no deviation, plunged into a wood, and reappeared just at the summit of the pass, perhaps a quarter of a mile further. It is the point where the Ordnance map marks a height of feet, and where one finally leaves the valley of the Itchen to enter that of the Wey.

The complexity of this corner is best understood in the sketch-map on the following page.

At the point where the Old Road leaves the wood, it merges again into the London turnpike, which turns its direction (as the map shows) so as to correspond with the direction of the Old Road. This identity between the prehistoric and the modern is maintained nearly as far as Alton, and, if we

The Old Road

except a short gap before that town, the coincidence of the Old Road and some existing highway may be said to continue right on to Puttenham, a distance of seventeen miles.

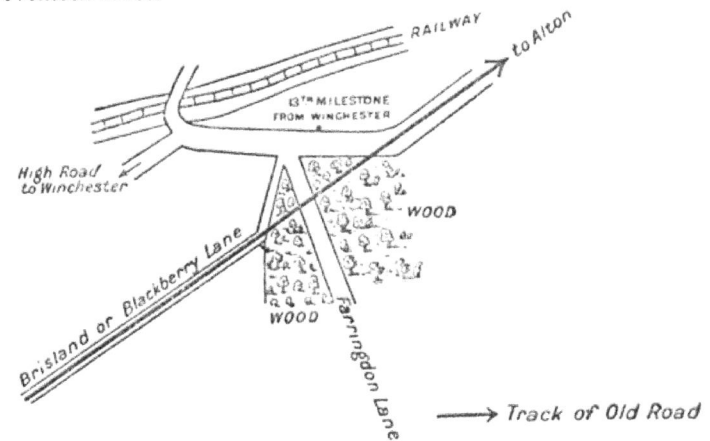

[Map showing: RAILWAY, to Alton, 13TH MILESTONE FROM WINCHESTER, High Road to Winchester, Brisland or Blackberry Lane, WOOD, Farringdon Lane, Track of Old Road]

The valley which now opened eastward under the dull morning light reminded me of one of those noble dales which diversify the long slope of the Chiltern Hills. Like them it had the round sweep of the Chalk; beeches, the trees of the Chalk, adorned it; its direction was the same, its dryness, its neat turf; but it lacked the distant horizons.

For two miles the road, magnificent in surface and in breadth, one of the finest in England, followed the bottom of the valley, falling in that distance some feet; and in all this part it was most evidently the oldest of ways across these hills. There could be repeated of it what has been said above with regard to the road between Bishop Sutton and Ropley, and what will appear further on in the valley of the Wey: that any track, ancient or modern, was bound to follow the same course. For the dry and porous soil permitted a journey even under the earliest conditions along the lowest points, and, so permitted, such a journey had the advantage of descending by the easiest gradient. Had it taken to the hillside it would have fallen at last upon Alton by way of a steep spur. Moreover, the bottom of the valley is here constant in direction, not curving as we had found it on the far side of the watershed, and this direction deviates little from the straight line to Alton.

These characters do not attach to the London turnpike after the fifteenth milestone is passed; it turns somewhat sharply to the right (or southward) and falls by a corner into the road from the Meon valley at the entry of Chawton village. Such a course one may be certain was not followed by the Old Road. It could not but have preserved the alignment which the valley had already given it, and which corresponds, moreover, with the High Street of Alton itself. For these seven furlongs there can be no doubt that it continued straight along the dip of the valley, and entered Alton on the northern side[] of the triangular common called 'The Butts,' by which one approaches the town from the south-west.

We were unable to prove this by direct examination; the main line of railway has here obliterated much by an embankment, and to this has been added all the new work of the Meon valley line, and the junction. The ground has therefore lost all its original character, and its oldest marks have disappeared. We made no attempt to follow the direct path for this short mile. We descended the high-road round by Chawton to Alton, and the first division of our task, the division in which a greater proportion of uncertainty would exist than in any other, was accomplished.

Comforted by such a thought, we drank mild ale at the 'Three Tuns' for about half an hour.

Alton to Shalford
Twenty-one miles

At Alton, with the green by which one enters the town from the west, begins a stretch of the Old Road, which stands by itself.

It may be roughly called the division between Alton and Farnham, but it stretches for a mile or two beyond Farnham to the pond at Whiteways, where the main road climbs the summit of the Hog's Back, and leaves the Pilgrim's Way a few hundred yards to the south.

This section, just over thirteen miles in length, has several peculiarities which distinguish it from the rest of the Road.

First—It follows the river Wey for miles, not as it followed the river Itchen, on a dry ledge above the stream, but right along the low land of the waterside. This is a feature in the Old Road not to be discovered in any other part of its course. It takes care to be within easy reach of water for men and horses, but it avoids the low level of a stream, and thick cover and danger of floods which such a level usually threaten. We had not found it (save for a very few yards) in immediate touch with the Itchen, nor should we find it later on running by the Mole, the Darent, or the Medway. Even the Stour, whose valley it is compelled to follow, it regards from heights well above the river.

Secondly—It runs for a part of this division upon clay, a soil which elsewhere it carefully avoids as being about the worst conceivable for a primitive and unmetalled road. Elsewhere (after Wrotham, for instance), it will make a detour rather than attempt any considerable stretch of gault; but here, for several miles along this valley of the Wey, it faces the danger.

Thirdly—In every other portion of its long journey it passes along the *edge* of habitations and tilled land; it was brought to do so by the same economic tendency which makes our railways to-day pass by the edges, not the centre of most towns; but here it must often have run right through whatever cultivation existed; at Alton, at Farnham, and in one village between, Bentley, it forms the high street of the place. A track which carefully just avoids Guildford, Dorking, Reigate, Westerham, Wrotham, Charing, and a dozen smaller places here touches and occasionally passes through the earliest groups of houses, the earliest pastures and ploughed fields.

Finally, there is a correspondence between it and the modern high-road for the *whole* of this considerable distance of over thirteen miles. In this character, again, the division we were now entering is unique.

We have indeed already found it identical with a modern road. The modern high-road also corresponds with the old way for something like a mile at Otford over the Darent, and for two or three miles beyond; it is a modern road for more than half a mile before you reach the ferry at Snodland, and there is a road in construction which follows its track for some hundreds of yards on Gravelly Hill, near Caterham. For many miles of its course it is identical if not with high-roads at least with metalled lanes, as we had already found between Itchen Stoke and Bishop Sutton, and very commonly with unmetalled tracks or paths. But in all these cases it is broken: there are stretches of it unused. Modern advantages and modern necessities have left the Old Road continually to one side. Here for this very considerable distance it is identical with the great turnpike, and so remains identical up to and beyond its point of junction with the older 'Harrow Way' at Farnham.

Can we discover any explanation for this coincidence of a prehistoric track with the high-road of our own time, which is almost indifferent to soil? for the crossing of the clay? for the neighbourhood of the river?

A little consideration will enable us to do so. The hills which everywhere else afford so even a platform for the prehistoric road are here of a contour which forbids their use. To-day, as a thousand years ago, any road down this valley must have run upon this lowest line.

The contour-lines, of which a rough sketch is here appended, are enough to prove it.

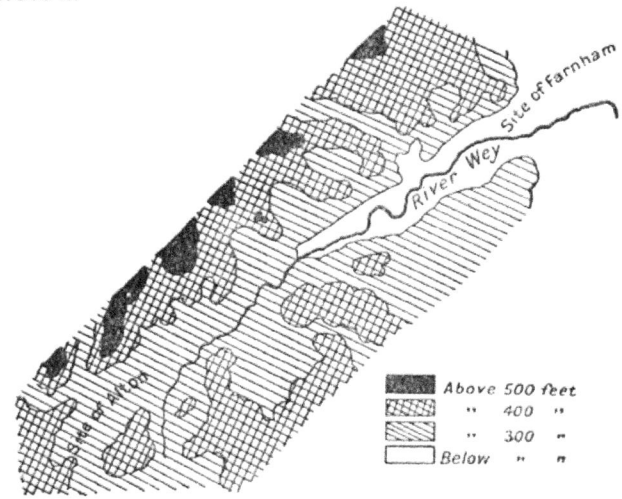

There is a deep combe at Holybourne Down, two more on either side of Froyle, a fourth beyond Bentley, a fifth—smaller—before Farnham. All these gullies cut up into a hopeless tangle what in Surrey and Kent will become one unbroken bank of chalk. Any path attempting these hillsides would either have doubled its length in avoiding the hollows, or would—had it remained direct—

have been a succession of steep ascents and falls; all the dry slopes which bound the vale to the north are a succession of steep and isolated projections, thrust out from the distant main chain of the chalk; many of them are crowned with separated summits. The road is therefore compelled to follow the valley floor with all the consequences I have noted.

As far as Froyle, two and a half miles from Alton, it never leaves the river by more than a quarter of a mile, but the valley is here dry, the soil gravelly and sandy, the height considerable (above three hundred feet), and there is no reason why it should go further from the stream than it did in the valley of the Itchen. After Froyle you get the clay, and then right on through Bentley the road does attempt to get away northward from the stream, avoiding the marshy levels and keeping to the -feet contour-line. It does not approach the river again till firmer ground is found near the Bull Inn. Thence to within two miles of Farnham it has to negotiate a good deal of clay, but it picks out such patches of gravel as it can find,[] and it must be remembered that the valley of the Wey, in this early part, drains more rapidly, and has a less supply of water than that of the Itchen. Near Farnham, somewhat beyond Runwick House, it finds the sand again, and can follow along the low level without difficulty.

The Old Road keeps throughout this passage to the sunny northern bank of the river, so that, while it is compelled to keep to the bottom of the valley, it attempts at least to get the driest part of it.

Farnham, at the mouth of this valley, the point of junction between the Old Road and its still older predecessor from Salisbury Plain, was always a place of capital importance, especially in war. The Roman entrenchment, two miles up the valley, the Roman dwellings to the south, tell us only a little of its antiquity; and though our knowledge of the castle extends no further than the eleventh century, the fact that it was the meeting-place of the roads that came from Salisbury Plain, from the Channel, from London, and from the Straits of Dover, necessarily made it a key to southern England.

We have seen how the western roads converge there, first the Harrow Way, then our own road from Southampton Water and Winchester (a road which probably received the traffic of all the south beyond Dorsetshire), then the road from Portsmouth and the Meons, which came in at Chawton.

The accident of the Surrey hills made all men who wished to get to the south-western ports from the Thames valley and the east pass through Farnham. Travellers going west and north from the Weald were equally compelled, if they would avoid the ridge, to pass through Farnham. The former had to come down north of the Hog's Back, the latter from the south of it, and it was ever at Farnham that they met.

At Farnham, therefore, the first political division of our road may be said to end; and after Farnham the western tracks, now all in one, proceed to the Straits of Dover, or rather to Canterbury, which is the rallying-point of the several Kentish ports.

Just outside the town the road begins to rise: it is an indication that the road is about to take the flank of the hills, a position which it holds uninterruptedly (save for four short gaps occasioned by four river valleys) from this point until the Camp above Canterbury.

Hitherto, for reasons which I have explained, the road has had no opportunity of this kind. The hills of the Itchen valley were not sufficiently conspicuous, those of the upper Wey too tortuous, for the trail to take advantage of a dry, even, and well-drained slope. The height to which it rises between Ropley and Alton is not a height chosen for its own purpose, but a height which had to be overcome of necessity to cross the watershed. Henceforward, until we were within a few miles of Canterbury, there stretched before us, on and on, day after day, the long line of the northern heights, whose escarpment presented everything the Old Road needed for its foundation, and of which I have written at such length in the earlier portion of this book.

The rise continued gently until the inn at Rumbold was passed, and the fork at Whiteways was reached. Here the old flanking road went up along the ridge of the Hog's Back in the shape of the modern turnpike, while our track was left to continue its eastward way, two hundred feet below, upon the side of the hill.

Its soil was here a thin strip of the green-sand which continued to support us, until next day we crossed the Tillingbourne, just above Shere. It runs, therefore, firmly and evenly upon a dry soil, and the villages and the churches mark its ancient progress.

The afternoon was misty, even the telegraph poles, which at first marked the ridge of the Hog's Back above us, disappeared in the first half mile. We went unhappily and in the fog regretting the baker's cart which had taken us along many miles of road so swiftly and so well: a cart of which I have not spoken any more than I have of the good taverns we sat in, or of the curious people we met (as for instance, the warrior at Farnham), because they are not germane to such an historical essay as is this.

We went, I say, regretting the baker's cart, and came to the wonderful church of Seale standing on its little mound. We noted that the track passed to southward of it, not right against its southern porch, but as near as it could get, given the steep accident of the soil just beyond. We noted this (but dully, for we were very tired), and we plodded on to Shoelands.

We were in the thick of the memories which are the last to hang round the Old Road, I mean the memories of those pilgrims, who, after so many thousand years of its existence, had luckily preserved the use and trace of the way.

Seale was built at the expense of Waverley, right in the enthusiasm that followed the first pilgrimages, just after . The names also of the hamlets have been held to record the pilgrimage. How Seale (a name found elsewhere just off the Old Road) may do so I cannot tell. 'Shoelands' has been connected with 'Shooling'—almsgiving. Compton church itself was famous. Even little Puttenham had its pilgrim's market, and Shalford its great fair, called Becket's fair. We left Seale then, and at last, two miles on and very weary, we approached Puttenham, where, for the first time since Alton, something of exploration awaited us.

There was, indeed, just before reaching Puttenham, a small difficulty, but it is not of this that I am writing. The Old Road, which had for miles coincided with

The Old Road

the lane, turned a sharp corner, and this, as I have already remarked, is so much against its nature in every known part of it, that I could only ascribe it to a cultivated field[] which has turned the road. Once tillage had begun, the road would be led round this field, and the old track, crossing it diagonally, would disappear under the plough; the original way must have run much as is suggested at the point marked X upon the map, and the suggestion has the greater force from the presence of a footpath following this line.

But the point is of little importance and is easily settled. In Puttenham itself lay the more interesting problem, to elucidate which this sketch was drawn.

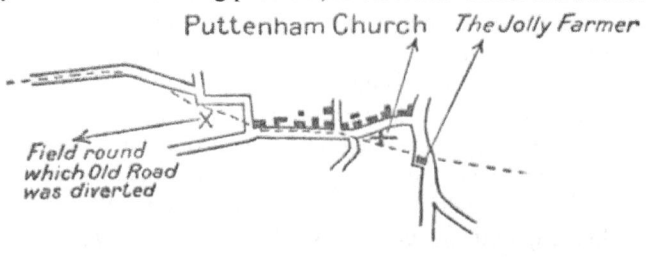

Puttenham Church — The Jolly Farmer

Field round which Old Road was diverted

— — — — Track of Old Road

It arises, just before the church is reached, and affords a very interesting example of how the Old Road has been lost and may be recovered.

The present road goes round to the north of the church, outside a high wall, which there forbids any passage. It turns sharp round a corner, and then proceeds due south to the village of Compton. When it has passed through this village, it turns north again, and so reaches St. Catherine's chapel, near which point it is agreed that the passage of the Wey was made.

Not only does the modern road take this circuitous course, but the pilgrims of the later Middle Ages probably followed a direction not very different. Compton church perhaps attracted them.

It is not the only place in which we shall find their leisurely piety misleading our research.

The Pilgrimage and the modern road both tend to make us miss the original track. That track, as a group of independent facts sufficiently show, passed south of Puttenham church, continuing the direction which it had hitherto followed from Seale; it went past the inn miscalled 'The Jolly Farmer,' and so on in a straight line over Puttenham Heath, where it is still marked by a rough cart-track kind of way.

One must here repeat an argument which continually recurs in these pages. Short of a physical obstacle, there is no reason but private property, and property long established and well defined, to give rise to such an unnatural halt in a path as is here made by a sudden turn of a right angle.

We know that the enclosure of this church within the wall was comparatively recent.

We know that in every case where the Old Road passes directly past a village church, it passes to the south. From the south, as we have already seen, the entry of the traveller was made; for, to repeat the matter, a custom presumably much older than our religion, gave approach to sacred places from the side of the sun.

The face of the Inn, the road before it (ending now abruptly and without meaning at the wall), and the road through Puttenham village are all in the same alignment.

It is an alignment that makes for the passage of the Wey (for Shalford, that is), much in the direction the Old Road has held since Seale.

The alignment is continued on through Puttenham Heath by an existing track, and in all this continuous chain there is no break, save the comparatively modern wall round the church.

Finally, Puttenham Heath had furnished antiquities of every sort, especially of the Neolithic period and of the Bronze: all within a small area, and all in the immediate neighbourhood of this Way.

So many indications were sufficient to make us follow the right-of-way across Puttenham Heath, and our conjecture was confirmed by our finding at the further edge of the heath, a conspicuous embankment marked by an exact line of three very aged trees, which everywhere indicate the track.

Though it was hardly a road, rough and marked only by ruts in the winter soil and by its rank of secular trees, it was most evidently the Old Road. We were glad to have found it.

When we had passed through the hollow to the north of a few cottages, direct evidence of the road disappeared at the boundary of Monk's Hatch Park, but it was not lost for long. yards further on, laid on the same line, a slightly sunken way reappeared; it ran a few yards below the recently made Ash Path, and led directly by the lane along the south of Brixbury Wood, across the Compton Road, and so by a lane called 'Sandy Lane,' beyond, over the crest of the hill, till, as the descent began, it became metalled, grew wider, and merged at last into the regular highway which makes straight for St. Catherine's Hill and the ferry and ford below it.

ROUGH, AND MARKED ONLY BY RUTS IN THE WINTER SOIL, AND BY ITS RANK OF SECULAR TREES

The Old Road having thus coincided once more with a regular road, we went at a greater pace, observing little of our surroundings (since nothing needed to be discovered), and hoped to make before it was quite dark the passage of the river.

THAT CURIOUS PLATFORM WHICH SUPPORTS IN SUCH AN IMMENSE ANTIQUITY OF CONSECRATION THE RUINS OF ST. CATHERINE'S CHAPEL

Arrived, however, at that curious platform which supports in such an immense antiquity of consecration the ruins of St. Catherine's chapel, we saw that the exact spot at which the river was crossed was not easily to be determined. The doubt does not concern any considerable space. It hesitates between two points on the river, and leaves unmapped about yards of the road; but that gap is, it must be confessed, unsolved so far as our investigation could be carried.

It is certain that the prehistoric road begins again by the north-western corner of the Chantries Wood. Tradition and the unbroken trail hence to St. Martha's hill-top confirm it. The arguments I have used in the last few pages show equally that the road led, on this side of the way, up to the point below St. Catherine's chapel where we were now standing.

It is, moreover, extremely probable that the platform of St. Catherine's was the look-out from which the first users of this track surveyed their opportunities for passing the river, and near to it undoubtedly their successors must have beaten down the road.

The precipitous face towards the stream, the isolation of the summit and its position, commanding a view up and down the valley, render it just such a place as would, by its value for their journeys and their wars, have made it sacred to a tribe: its sanctity during the Middle Ages gives the guess a further credential. But in framing an hypothesis as to how the valley was taken from the descent of St. Catherine's to the rise at the Chantries beyond the stream, one is met by two sets of facts irreconcilable with one another, and supporting arguments each, unfortunately, of equal weight. These facts are few, simple, and urgent; they are as follows:—

Primitive man we must imagine chose, if he could, a ford, and kept to such a passage rather than to any form of ferry. The ford exists. It has given its name 'The Shallow Ford' to the village which grew up near it. The church stands close by. So far it would seem that the road certainly passed over the crest of St. Catherine's, came down to the south of that hill, crossed at Shalford, and reached the Chantries by that passage.

On the other hand a sunken way of great antiquity leads directly from St. Catherine's Hill down to the river. It follows the only practicable descent of the bank. It is in line with the previous trend of the Old Road; at its foot is a ferry which has had a continuous history at least as old as the pilgrimage, and beyond this ferry, the path over the field, and the avenue beyond the main road, lead immediately and without any diversion to that point at the foot of the Chantries Hill where, as I have said, the Old Road is again evident.

From Shalford no such track is apparent, nor could it be possible for a passage by Shalford to be made, save at the expense of a detour much sharper than the Old Road executes in any other part of its course.

In the face of these alternatives no certain decision could be arrived at. The medieval route was here no guide, for it had already left the road to visit Compton, and was free to use Shalford ford, the ferry, or even Guildford Bridge—all three of which the pilgrims doubtless passed indifferently, for all three were far older than the pilgrimage.

It may be that the ferry stands for an old ford, now deepened. It may be that the passage at Shalford was used first, and soon replaced by that of the ferry. We knew of no discoveries in that immediate neighbourhood which might have helped us to decide; we were compelled, though disappointed, to leave the point open.

It was now quite dark. My companion and I clambered down the hill, stole a boat which lay moored to the bank, and with a walking-stick for an oar painfully traversed the river Wey. When we had landed, we heard, from the further bank, a woman, the owner of the boat, protesting with great violence.

We pleaded our grave necessity; put money in the boat, and then, turning, we followed the marshy path across the field to the highway, and when we reached it, abandoned the Old Road in order to find an inn.

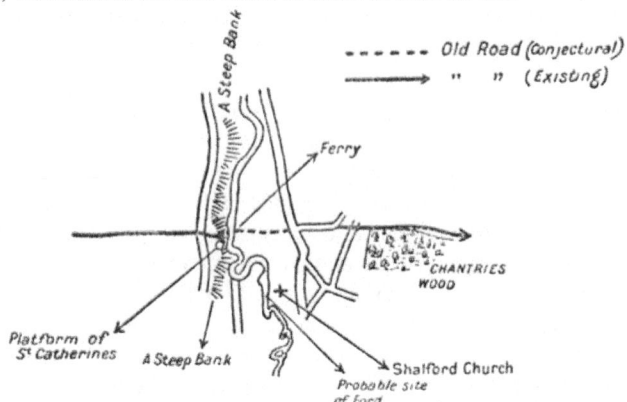

[Map showing: Old Road (Conjectural) – – – – – –; Old Road (Existing) ——→; A Steep Bank; Ferry; CHANTRIES WOOD; Platform of St Catherines; A Steep Bank; Shalford Church; Probable site of ford]

We slept that night at Guildford, whence the next morning, before daylight, we returned up the highway to the spot where we had left the Old Road, and proceeded through the gate and up the avenue to follow and discover that section of the road between the Wey and the Mole which is by far the richest in evidences of prehistoric habitation—a stretch of the Old Road which, partly from its proximity to London, partly from its singular beauty, partly from its accidental association with letters, but mainly from the presence of rich and leisured men, has been hitherto more fully studied than any other, and which yet provides in its sixteen miles more matter for debate than any other similar division between Winchester and Canterbury.

Shalford to Dorking Pits
Eleven miles

The Old Road leaves the Guildford and Shalford highway on the left, or east, in a line with the path which has reached it from the ferry. We passed through a gate and entered an avenue of trees, at the end of which the newer road which has been built along it turns off to the left, while the Old Road itself, in the shape of a vague lane, begins to climb the hill. The light was just breaking, and we could follow it well.

At this point, and for some distance further, it is known to historians and antiquaries, and preserves, moreover, many indications of that use whereby the medieval pilgrimage revived and confirmed its course. It skirts by the side of, and finally passes through, woods which still bear the name of the 'Chantries,' and climbs to that isolated summit where stands the chapel of St. Thomas: 'the

Martyr's' chapel, which, in the decay of religion and corruption of tradition, came to be called 'St. Martha's.'

This spot, for all its proximity to London and to the villas of the rich, preserves a singular air of loneliness. It has a dignity and an appeal which I had thought impossible in land of which every newspaper is full; and that morning, before men were stirring, with the mist all about us and the little noises of animals in the woods, we recovered its past. The hill responded to the ancient camps, just southward and above us. It responded to its twin height of St. Catherine's: the whole landscape had forgotten modern time, and we caught its spirit the more easily that it relieved us of our fears lest in this belt near London the Old Road should lose its power over us.

It has been conjectured, upon such slight evidence as archæology possesses, that the summit was a place of sacrifice. Certainly great rings of earth stood here before the beginning of history; certainly it was the sacred crown for the refugees of Farley Heath, of Holmbury, of Anstie Bury, and of whatever other stations of war may have crowned these defiant hills.

If it saw rites which the Catholic Church at last subdued, we know nothing of them; we possess only that thread of tradition which has so rarely been broken in western Europe: the avenue, whereby, until the sixteenth century, all our race could look back into the very origins of their blood.

The hill was an isolated peak peculiar and observable. Such separate heights have called up worship always wherever they were found: the Middle Ages gave this place what they gave to the great outstanding rocks of the sea, the 'St. Michaels': to the dominating or brooding capitols of cities, Montmartre or Our Lady of Lyons; perhaps Arthur's Seat had a shrine. The Middle Ages gave it what they had inherited, for they revered the past only, they sought in the past their ideals, and hated whatever might destroy the common memory of the soil and the common observances of men—as modern men hate pain or poverty.

Remembering all this we rested at the chapel on the hill-top, and considered it wearily. We regretted its restoration to new worship, and recollected (falsely, as it turned out) famous graves within it.

The air was too hazy to distinguish the further view to the south. The Weald westward was quite hidden, and even the height of Hirst Wood above and beyond us eastward was hardly to be seen.

When we had spent half an hour at this place we prepared to go down the further side, but first we looked to see whether the Old Road passed clearly to one side or the other of the summit, for we thought that matter would be of importance to us as a guide for its direction in similar places later on. But we could decide nothing. Certainly the track makes northward of the church until it is near the top of the hill, but, as it gets near, it points right at it (as we might expect), is lost, and is only recovered some twenty or fifty yards beyond the platform of the summit, coming apparently neither from the south nor from the north of the church; the direction is a little obscured, moreover, by a modern plantation which confuses the beginning of the descent. Soon it grew clear enough, and we followed it at a race, down the hill perhaps half a mile. It was plainer and plainer as we went onward, till it struck the road which leads from Guildford to Albury.

Here there rises a difficulty unique in the whole course of the way. It is a difficulty we cannot pretend to have solved. The trail for once goes to the damp and northward side of a hill: the hill on which stands Weston Wood. It is an exception to an otherwise universal rule, and an exception for which no modern conditions can account.

There is apparently no reason why it should not have followed its otherwise invariable rule of taking the southerly slope, and it could have chosen the dry clean air of the heath and kept all the way near the fresh water of the Tillingbourne. On the other hand, there is no doubt whatever of its direction. Tradition, the existence of modern tracks, and more important still, the direction of the road after it leaves St. 'Martha's' chapel, all point to the same conclusion. The Pilgrim's Way crosses diagonally the field beyond the main road, goes just behind the little cottage at its corner,[] and then makes for Albury Park by way of a wretched and difficult sunken lane to the north of Weston Wood. We entered this neglected and marshy way. It was a place of close, dark, and various trees, full of a damp air, and gloomy with standing water in the ruts: the whole an accident differing in tone from all that we knew of the road, before and after.

It was not long in passing. We left the undergrowth for the open of a field, and found the trace of the road pointing to the wall of Albury Park. It entered just north of the new church, and then followed a clearly marked ridge upon which, here and there, stood the yews.

A PLACE OF CLOSE DARK AND VARIOUS TREES, FULL OF A DAMP AIR, AND GLOOMY WITH STANDING WATER-RUTS

After the Old Road enters Albury Park there is a doubtful section of about a mile and a half. The -inch Ordnance for Surrey (revised eight years ago) carries the track southward at a sharp angle, round the old church of SS. Peter and Paul and then along the south of Shere till it stops suddenly at a farm called 'Gravel Pits Farm.' It seemed to us as we overlooked the valley from the north, that the Old Road followed a course now included in the garden of Albury, and corresponding, perhaps, to the Yew Walk which Cobbett has rendered famous, and so reached the ford which crosses the Tillingbourne at the limits of the park—a ford still called 'Chantry' ford, and evidently the primitive crossing-place of the stream.

Thence it probably proceeded, as we did, along that splendid avenue of limes which is the mark of the village of Shere. But from the end of this there are some three hundred yards of which one cannot be very certain. It comes so very near to the church that one may presume, without too much conjecture, that it passed beside the southern porch. If it did so, it should have crossed the stream again near where the smithy stands to-day, and this double crossing of the stream may be accounted for by the presence of a shrine and of habitation in the oldest times. But if the bridge be taken as an indication (which bridges often are) of the original place where the stream was re-crossed, then the track would have left the church on the right, and would have curved round to become the present high-road to Gomshall. Nothing certain can be made of its passage here, except that the track marked upon the Ordnance map will not fit in with the character of the road. The Ordnance map loses it at Gomshall, finds it again much further on, having turned nearly a right angle and going (for no possible reason) right up to and over the crest of the hills: across Ranmore Common and so to Burford Bridge. The first part of this cannot but be a confusion with the Old Drove Road to London. As for the crossing of the Mole at Burford Bridge we shall see in a moment that the medieval pilgrimage passed the river at this point, but the prehistoric road at a point a mile and more up stream.

Taking into consideration the general alignment of the Old Road, its 'habits,' the pits that mark it, and its crossing-place in the Mole valley, we did not doubt that we should find it again on the hillside beyond Gomshall.

THAT SPLENDID AVENUE OF LIMES

Its track must have crossed the high-road at a point nearly opposite Netley House, and by a slow climb have made for the side of the Downs and for the chalk, which henceforward it never leaves, save under the necessity of crossing a river valley, until it reaches Chilham, sixty miles away.

Beyond the grounds of Netley House the Old Road is entirely lost. A great ploughed field has destroyed every trace of it, but the direction is quite easy to follow when one notes the alignment which it pursues upon its reappearance above the line of cultivation. It must have run, at first, due north-west, and turned more and more westward as it neared Colekitchen Lane: it must have crossed the mouth of Colekitchen Combe, which here runs into the hills, and have reached in this fashion the -feet contour-line at the corner of Hacklehurst Down, where we come on it just at the far edge of the Combe, on the shoulder about three hundred yards east of the rough lane which leads up from under the railway arch to the Downs.[]

From this point we could follow it mile after mile without any difficulty. Its platform is nearly always distinct; the yews follow it in a continual procession, though it is cut here and there by later roads. The old quarries and chalk pits which mark it henceforward continually along the way to Canterbury begin to appear, and it does not fail one all along the hill and the bottom of Denbies Park until, at the end of that enclosure, it is lost in the pit of the Dorking Lime Works. It does not reappear. Beyond there is a considerable gap—nearly a mile in length—before it can reach the river Mole, which it must cross in order to pursue its journey. With this gap I shall deal in a moment, but it was the affair of our next day's journey, for short as had been the distance from Shalford, the many checks and the seeking here and there which they had entailed had exhausted the whole of the short daylight. The evening had come when we stood on the Down looking over to Box Hill beyond.

From thence across the valley, Box Hill attracted and held the sight as one looked eastward: the strongest and most simple of our southern hills. It stood out like a cape along our coasting journey, our navigation of the line of the Downs. The trend of the range is here such that the clean steep of this promontory hides the slopes to the east. It occupies the landscape alone.

It has been debated and cannot be resolved, why these great lines of chalk north and south of the Weald achieve an impression of majesty. They are not very high. Their outline is monotonous and their surface bare. Something of that economy and reserve by whose power the classic in verse or architecture grows upon the mind is present in the Downs. These which we had travelled that day were not my own hills—Duncton and Bury, Westburton, Amberley and all—but they were similar because they stood up above the sand and the pines, and because they were of that white barren soil, clothed in close turf, wherein nothing but the beech, the yew, and our own affection can take root and grow.

At the end of a day's work, a short winter day's, it was possible to separate this noble mark of what was once a true county of Surrey; to separate it even in the mind, from the taint of our time and the decay and vileness which hang like a smell of evil over whatever has suffered the influence of our great towns. The advancing darkness which we face restored the conditions of an older time; the staring houses merged with the natural trees; a great empty sky and a river mist gave the illusion of a place unoccupied.

It was possible to see the passage of the Mole as those rare men saw it who first worked their way eastward to the Straits, and had not the suggestion seemed too fantastic for a sober journey of research, one might have taken the appeal of the hills for a kind of guide; imagining that with such a goal the trail would plunge straight across the valley floor to reach it.

By more trustworthy methods, the track of the Old Road was, as I have said, less ascertainable. Presumably it followed, down the shoulder of the hill, a spur leading to the river, but the actual mark of the road was lost, its alignment soon reached ploughed land; nothing of the place of crossing could be determined till the stream itself was examined, nor indeed could we make sure of the true point until we found ourselves unexpectedly aided by the direction of the road when we recovered it upon the further bank. This we left for the dawn of the next day; and so went down into Dorking to sleep.

I have said that from Denbies, or rather from the pits of Dorking Lime Works, the path is apparently lost. It reappears, clearly enough marked, along the lower slope of Box Hill, following the -feet contour-line; but between the two points is a gap extending nearly a mile on one side of the river and almost half a mile upon the other.

I have seen it conjectured that the Old Road approached the Mole near Burford, and that it turned sharply up over Ranmore Common on its way. That it crossed Ranmore Common is impossible. Undoubtedly a prehistoric track ran over that heath, but it was a branch track to the Thames—one of the many 'feeders' which confuse the record of the Old Road. But that it crossed at Burford Bridge is arguable.

The name Burford suggests the crossing of the river. The pilgrims undoubtedly passed here, going down Westhumble Lane, and using the bridge—for everybody uses a bridge once it has been built. Thence they presumably followed along the western flank of Box Hill, and so round its base to that point where, as I have said, the embankment and the old trees reappear.

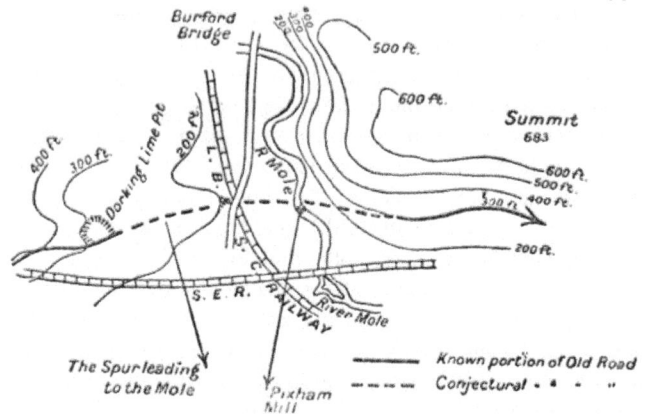

[Figure: Map showing Burford Bridge, River Mole, S.E.R. Railway, Dorking Lime Pit, Pixham Mill, contour lines from 100 ft to 600 ft, Summit 683. Legend: Known portion of Old Road; Conjectural. The Spur leading to the Mole.]

Nevertheless, those who imagine that the original road, the prehistoric track, followed this course, were, we thought, in error. We had little doubt that, after the lime pit outside Denbies Park, the road followed down the moderate shoulder or spur which here points almost directly eastward towards the valley, crossed the railway just north of the road bridge over the line, approached the Mole at a point due east of this, and immediately ascended the hill before it to that spot where it distinctly reappears: a spot near the -feet contour-line somewhat to the west of the lane leading from the Reigate Road to the crest of the hills.[]

IT STOOD OUT LIKE A CAPE ALONG OUR COASTING JOURNEY, OUR NAVIGATION OF THE LINE OF THE DOWNS

I will give my reasons for this conclusion.

A diversion round by Burford Bridge would have taken the early travellers far out of their way. Roughly speaking, they would have had to go along two sides of an equilateral triangle instead of its base: three miles for one and a half. Now, had they any reason to do this? None that I can see. Wherever, in crossing a valley, the Old Road diverges from its general alignment, it diverges either to avoid bad soil or to find a ford. The name Burford would suggest to those who have not carefully examined the river that this diversion might have been made necessary in order to find a shoal at that point; but the Mole is very unlike the other streams south of the Thames. It disappears into 'swallows': it 'snouzles,' and there is a theory that the river got its name from this habit of burrowing underground. At almost any one of these numerous 'swallows' the river can quite easily be crossed, and a considerable diminution of its stream, though perhaps not a true 'swallow,' is to be found at the point I indicate.

Again, that all-important consideration in a new country—I mean the dryness of the soil over which a road passes—was very much helped by taking the more direct of the two lines. Ground with some slope to it, and always fairly dry, comes here on either side, close to the river. But down by Burford, on the western side, there is quite a little plain, which must have been marshy, and for all I know, may be so still. Moreover, we shall find further on at Otford, and at Snodland, that the Old Road in crossing a valley always chooses a place where some spur of high land leads down to the river and corresponds to a dry rise immediately upon the other bank. Coupled with the fact that a direction such as I suggest makes a natural link between the two known parts of the road, being very nearly in one alignment with them, and remembering that Burford Bridge was built in connection with a very much later Roman way northward up the valley (it is evidently the Bridge of the Stane Street), that its direction and the place at which it crosses are obviously dependent on a north and south road, not on an east and west one, we decided to approach the eastern bank, and to see whether any existing trace of a road would support what seemed to us the most tenable hypothesis.

It cannot be pretended that any very distinct evidence clinched what remains, after all, our mere theory; but there was enough to convince us, at least, and I believe to convince most people, who will do as we did, and stand upon the Old Road at the base of Box Hill looking towards Denbies on the other side of the valley. He will see, following a very obvious course, a certain number of yews of great age, remaining isolated in the new-ploughed land. These, leading across the river, are continued at a very slight angle by a definite alignment of three trees, equally isolated though far less old, standing equally in comparatively modern cultivated land, and leading directly to the place where the track is lost at its exit from Denbies Park; and the whole line follows two spurs of land which approach the river from either side.

A conclusion thus reached cannot pretend to such a value as I would demand for the rest of our reconstructions: such as, for instance, can legitimately be demanded for the way in which we filled the gap at Puttenham. But it is far more convincing on the spot, and with the evidence before one (such as it is), than any verbal description can make it, and I would repeat that any one making the experiment with his own eyes will be inclined to agree with us.

When we had arrived at this decision in the first hour of daylight we turned eastward, and pursued our way by the raised and yew-lined track which was now quite unmistakable, and which we could follow for a considerable time without hesitation. It ran straight along the -feet contour-line, and took the southern edge of a wood called Brockham Warren.

Here for a short way we went through a stately but abandoned avenue, with the climbing woods up steep upon our left, and on our right a little belt of cover, through which the fall of the slope below us and the more distinct Weald and sandy hills could be seen in happy glimpses. When we came out upon the further side and found the open Down again, we had doubled (as it were) the Cape of Boxhill, and found ourselves in a new division of the road.

Boxhill to Titsey
Eighteen miles
After one turns the corner of Box Hill and enters this new division of the road is a great lime pit, which is called Betchworth Pit, and next to it a similar work, not quite as large, but huge enough to startle any one that comes upon it suddenly over the edge of the Downs. Between them they make up the chief landmark of the county.

We had already come across the first working of this kind shortly after we had recovered the Old Road beyond Gomshall, but that and the whole succeeding chain of pits were now disused, grown over with evergreens and damp enormous beeches. We had found a more modern excavation of the sort at the end of Denbies Park: it was called the Dorking Lime Works. Here, however, in these enormous pits, we came to something different and new. I looked up at their immensity and considered how often I had seen them through the haze: two patches of white shining over the Weald to where I might be lying on the crest of my own Downs, thirty miles away.

It is the oldest, perhaps, of the industries of England. Necessary for building, an excellent porous stratum in the laying of roads, the best of top-dressings for the stiff lands that lie just beneath in the valley, chalk and the lime burnt from it were among the first of our necessities.

Its value must have come even before stone building or made roads or the plough; it furnished the flints which were the first tools and weapons; it ran very near by the healthy green-sand where our earliest ancestors built their huts all along the edges of their hunting-ground, the Weald, on ridges now mostly deserted, and dark for the last three hundred years with pines.

The chalk, which I have spoken of coldly when I discussed the preservation of the Old Road, should somewhere be warmly hymned and praised by every man who belongs to south England, for it is the meaning of that good land. The sand is deserted since men learnt to plough; the Weald, though so much of its forest has fallen, is still nothing but the Weald—clay, and here and there the accursed new towns spreading like any other evil slime. But the chalk is our landscape and our proper habitation. The chalk gave us our first refuge in war by permitting those vast encampments on the summits. The chalk filtered our drink for us and built up our strong bones; it was the height from the slopes of which our villages, standing in a clear air, could watch the sea or the plain; we carved it—when it was hard enough; it holds our first ornaments; our clear streams run over it; the shapes and curves it takes and the kind of close rough grass it bears (an especial grass for sheep), are the cloak of our counties; its lonely breadths delight us when the white clouds and the flocks move over them together; where the waves break it into cliffs, they are the characteristic of our shores, and through its thin coat of whitish mould go the thirsty roots of our three trees—the beech, the holly, and the yew. For the clay and the sand might be deserted or flooded and the South Country would still remain, but if the Chalk Hills were taken away we might as well be the Midlands.

These pits which uncover the chalk bare for us show us our principal treasure and the core of our lives, and show it us in grand façades, steep down, taking the place of crags and bringing into our rounded land something of the stern and the abrupt. Every one brought up among the chalk pits remembers them more vividly than any other thing about his home, and when he returns from some exile he catches the feeling of his boyhood as he sees them far off upon the hills.

Therefore I would make it a test for every man who boasted of the South Country, Surrey men (if there are any left), and Hampshire men, and men of Kent (for they must be counted in): I would make it a test to distinguish whether they were just rich nobodies playing the native or true men to see if they could remember the pits. For my part I could draw you every one in my country-side even now. Duncton, where the little hut is, surrounded by deep woods, Amberley, Houghton, which I have climbed with a Spaniard, and where twice the hounds have gone over and have been killed, Mr. Potter's pit, down which we hunted a critic once, the pit below Whiteways, Bury Pit, and Burpham, and all the older smaller diggings, going back to the beginning, and abandoned now to ivy and to trees.

I know them and I love them all. The chalk gives a particular savour to the air, and I have found it good to see it caked upon my boots after autumn rains, or feel it gritty on my hands as I spread them out, coming in to winter fires.

All this delays me on the Old Road, but the pits can be given a meaning, even in research such as that upon which we were engaged.

The chalk hills, from Betchworth here right on to the Medway, have many such bites taken out of them by man, and there is this peculiarity about them, that very many of them cut into and destroy the Old Road.

I think it not fantastic to find for such a repeated phenomenon an explanation which also affords a clue to difficult parts of the way. The Old Road being originally the only track along these hills was necessarily the base of every pit that should be dug. Along it alone could the chalk be carried, or the lime when it was baked, and it was necessary for the Britons, the Romans, and their successors to make the floor of the lime pit upon a level with this track. Later when the valley roads were developed and the Old Road was no longer continuously used, it was profitable to sink the cutting further, below the level of the Old Road, and, indeed, as far as the point where the chalk comes to mix with the sand or clay of the lower level. As the Old Road grew more and more neglected the duty of protecting it was forgotten, and the exploitation of the pits at last destroyed it at these points.

Nevertheless, its line was quite easy to recover, across these Betchworth pits, though they are the largest cuttings in the county; later on we found no difficulty across the smaller ones near Otford and at Merstham. It is even true that the pits afforded a guide in one or two cases where we were in doubt what path to follow, and that our hypothesis according to which the pits naturally arose upon the track of the Old Road confirmed itself by discovering the way to us in more than one ambiguity.

Portions of the road remain even along the great Betchworth pits. These portions reappear at the same level, wherever the pits have left a crag of the old hillside standing, and when one gets to the point just above Betchworth station and to the cottages of the workmen, the path reappears quite plainly. It follows the hillside at a level of about feet, falls slightly below this contour-line to round the projecting spur of Brockham Hill, comes down to the high-road (the main road to London through Tadworth), follows it a couple of hundred yards, and leaves it to climb the hill at a point just south of the place where the -inch Ordnance map marks the height of feet.[]

Here there is a combe known as 'Pebble Combe.' The Old Road does not go round the combe but straight across its mouth, and begins to assume a character so new as to perplex us for a considerable time in our search. We did not understand the nature of the change until we had very carefully traced the path for more than another mile.

I will explain the difficulty.

The escarpment of the hills is here extremely steep. It falls at an angle which could not conveniently support a road, or at least could not support it without such engineering work as primitive men would have been incapable of performing, and this steep bit lasts without interruption from just east of Pebble Combe right away to the height above Reigate which is known as Quarry Hill.

Now, if the road could not be supported upon the bank of the escarpment, and yet desired—as it always must—to escape the damp land of the lower levels, it was bound to seek the crest. Nowhere hitherto in all this march from Winchester had we found it attempting the summits of the hills, but there were here unmistakable evidences that it was going to approach those summits and to keep to them as long as the steepness of the escarpment lasted.

Our inexperience made us hesitate a long while; but at last we saw, in a line of old yews above us, an indication that the hill was to be climbed, and on going up close to those yews we found that they ran along a platform which was the trodden and levelled mark of the Old Road, running here in a form precisely similar to that which we had found round Box Hill.

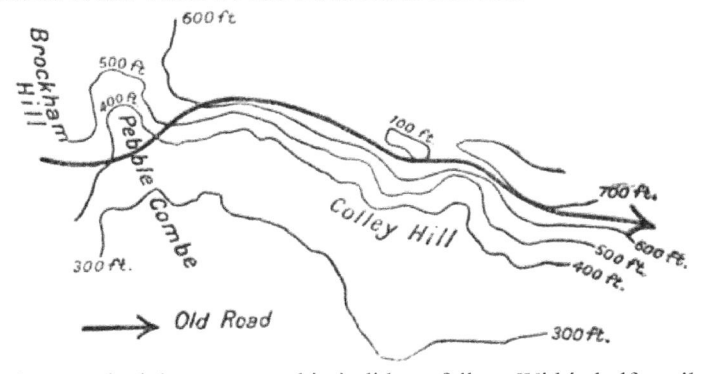

[Sketch map showing Brockham Hill, Pebble Combe, Colley Hill with contour lines at 300ft, 400ft, 500ft, 600ft, 700ft, 800ft, and the Old Road marked by an arrow.]

Once we had thus recovered it, it did not fail us. Within half a mile it climbed sideways along the hillside from that point, feet above the sea, which I have mentioned, to the neighbourhood of the -feet contour-line which here marks the edge of the range; and this line it follows with a slight rise corresponding to the rise of the crest all the way to what are known as the Buckland Hills, and the high knot which just tops the feet near Margery Wood.[]

To the north and to the south of this, at Walton Heath on the plateau above, and at Colley Farm in the valley below, there had been discoveries of Roman and of pre-Roman things; but though they pointed to its neighbourhood, these relics would not of themselves have given us the exact line of the road; that was furnished by the broad and unmistakable track which it had itself impressed upon the chalk from the usage of so many hundred years.

It was slow work here. Much of it ran through dense brushwood, where one had to stoop and push aside the branches, and all of it was damp, shaded from the sun by the mass of old yews, and less well drained on this flat edge and summit than it is on the hillside where it usually hangs. But though it is a difficult two miles, the path is discoverable all the way.

With Margery Wood it reaches the -feet line, runs by what I fear was a private path through a newly-enclosed piece of property. We remembered to spare the garden, but we permitted ourselves a trespass upon this outer hollow trench in the wood which marked our way.

A magnificent bit of open ground, from which we saw below us the sandy hills, and beyond, the whole of the Weald, led us on to a point where the Old Road once again corresponds with a modern and usable, though unmetalled and very dirty lane. This is the lane which runs to the south of the park of Margery Hall. It skirts to the north the property recently acquired by the War Office, and when it has passed the War Office boundary-stone it is carried across the high-road from Reigate to London by a suspension bridge, which must surely be the only example in Europe of so modern an invention serving to protect the record of so remote a past. Nor would there be any need for such a suspension bridge had not the London Road in the early part of the nineteenth century been eased in its steepness by a deep cutting, to cross which the suspension bridge was made. That bridge, once passed, the road pointed straight to the lodge of Gatton, and pursued its way through that park to the further lodge upon the eastern side.[]

Here should be submitted some criticism of the rather vague way in which the place-names of this district have been used by those who had preceded us in the reconstruction of the Pilgrim's Way.

Reigate, which was Churchfell at the Conquest, has been imagined to take its later title from the Old Road. Now the name, like that of Riggate in the north country, means certainly the passage near the road; but Reigate lay well below in the valley.

True, the pilgrims, and many generations before them, must have come down to this point to sleep, as they came down night after night to so many other points, stretched along the low land below the Old Road in its upland course from the Wey to the Stour. So common a halting-place was it in the later Middle Ages that the centre of Reigate town, the place where the Town Hall now stands, held the chapel of St. Thomas from perhaps the thirteenth century to the Reformation. But Reigate no more than Maidstone, another station of the medieval pilgrimage, could have stood on the Old Road itself. It may be another track which gives Reigate its name. Some Roman by-way which may have run from Shoreham (which the experts do not believe to have been a port), right through the Weald to Reigate, and so to London.

AND BEYOND, THE WHOLE OF THE WEALD

It is possible that a way from the Portus Adurni[] to London ran here by Reigate and climbed the hill above; one of those fingers reaching to the ports of the south coast, of which the Stane Street, the Watling Street, and perhaps the fragment further east by Marden, are the remnants: moreover, in the existence of such a road I think one can solve the puzzle of Gatton.

Gatton, which is now some three or four houses and a church and a park, sent two members to Parliament, from the fifteenth century until the Reform Bill. It was therefore at some time, for some reason, a centre of importance, not necessarily for its population but as a gathering-place or a market, or a place from which some old town had disappeared. Indeed a local tradition of such a town survives. One may compare the place with that other centre, High Cross, where is now the lonely crossing of the Fosse Way and Watling Street in Leicestershire.

Now, what would have given this decayed spot its importance long ago? Most probably the crossing of an east and west road (the Old Road) with another going north and south, which has since disappeared.

The influence of vested interests (for Gatton Park fetched twice its value on account of this anachronism) preserved the representation in the hands of one man until the imperfect reform of seventy years ago destroyed the Borough.

There is another point in connection with the Pilgrim's Way at Gatton. For the second time since it has left Winchester it goes to the north of a hill. At Albury it did so, as my readers have seen, for some reason not to be explained. In every other case between here and Canterbury the explanation is simple. It goes north to avoid a prominent spur in the range and a re-entrant angle at the further side. The map which I append will make this point quite clear.

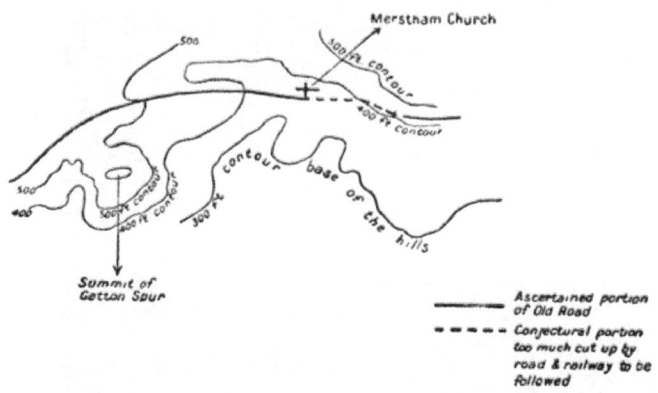

For precisely the same cause it goes north of the spur south of Caterham and much further on, some miles before Canterbury, it goes north of the spur in Godmersham Park.

We did not here break into another man's land, but were content to watch, from the public road outside, the line of the way as it runs through Gatton, and when we had so passed round outside the park we came to the eastern lodge, where the avenue runs on the line of the Old Road. Here the public lane corresponds to the Pilgrim's Way and passes by the land where was made a find of Roman and British coins, close to the left of the road.

After this point the road went gently down the ridge of the falling crest. This was precisely what we later found it doing at Godmersham, where also it climbs a crest and goes behind a spur, and having done so follows down the shoulder of the hill to the lower levels of the valley. The valley or depression cutting the hills after Gatton is the Merstham Gap, by which the main Brighton Road and the London and Brighton Railway cross the North Downs. The Old Road goes down to this gap by a path along the side of a field, is lost in the field next to it, but is recovered again just before the grounds of Merstham House; it goes straight on its way through these grounds, and passes south of Merstham House and just *south* of Merstham church; then it is suddenly lost in the modern confusion of the road and the two railway cuttings which lie to the east.

We left it there and went down to Merstham inn for food, and saw there a great number of horsemen all dressed alike, but of such an accent and manner that we could not for the life of us determine to what society they belonged. Only this was certain, that they were about to hunt some animal, and that this animal was not a fox. With reluctance we abandoned that new problem and returned to Merstham church to look for the road from the spot where it had disappeared.

So to have lost it was an annoyance and a disturbance, for the point was critical.

We had already learnt by our experience of the way between Dorking and Reigate, that when the escarpment is too steep to bear a track the Old Road will mount to the crest, and we saw before us, some two miles ahead, that portion of the Surrey hills known as Whitehill or (on the slopes) Quarry Hangers, where everything pointed to the road being forced to take the crest of the hill. The escarpment is there extremely steep, and is complicated by a number of sharp ridges with little intervening wedges of hollow, which would make it impossible for men and animals to go at a level halfway up the hillside. The Old Road then, certainly, had to get to the crest of these Downs before their steepness had developed. On the other hand the top of the crest was a stiff and damp clay which lasted up to the steep of Quarry Hangers.

The pilgrims of the Middle Ages probably went straight up the hill from Merstham by an existing track, got on to this clay, and followed Pilgrim's Lane along the crest—some shrine or house of call attracted them. The prehistoric road would certainly not have taken the clay in this fashion. On every analogy to be drawn from the rest of its course it would climb the hill at a slow slant, keeping to the chalk till it should reach the summit at some point where the clay had stopped and the slope below had begun to be steep. The problem before us was to discover by what line it climbed. And the beginning of the climb that would have given us the whole alignment was utterly lost, as I have said, in this mass of modern things, roads, railways, and cuttings, which we found just after Merstham church.

We walked along the road which leads to Rockshaw, and along which certain new villas have been built. We walked slowly, gazing all the time at the fields above us, to the north and the hillside, and searching for an indication of our path.

The first evidence afforded us was weak enough. We saw a line of hedge running up the hill diagonally near the -feet contour-line, and climbing slowly in such a direction as would ultimately point to the crest of the Quarry Hangers. Then we noticed the lime works, called on the map 'Greystone Lime Works,' which afforded us a further clue. We determined to make by the first path northward on to the hillside, and see if we could find anything to follow.

Such a path, leading near a cottage down a slight slope and the hill beyond, appeared upon our left when we had covered about three quarters of a mile of road from Merstham. We took it and reached the hedge of which I have spoken. Once there, although no very striking evidence was presented to us, there was enough to make us fairly certain of the way.

A continuous alignment of yew, hedge, and track, appeared behind us, coming straight, as it should do, from Merstham church and right *across* the old lime pit; before us it continued to climb diagonally the face of the hill. Lost under the plough in more than one large field, it always reappeared in sufficient lengths to be recognised, and gained the crest at last at a point which just missed the end of the clay, and was also just over the beginning of the Quarry Hangers steep.[]

Once arrived at the summit of Quarry Hangers we found the road to be quite clear: a neat embankment upon the turf; and when, half a mile beyond, we came to the cross-roads and the tower, we had reached a part of the Pilgrim's Way which, though short, had already been settled and did not need to detain us. It corresponds with the modern lane, goes just north of the spur known as Arthur's Seat (a spur upon the southern side of which stands a prehistoric camp), goes up over the summit of Gravelly Hill (where it is the same as a modern road now in the making), and at last strikes Godstone Woods just at the place where a boundary-stone marks the corner of another little patch of land belonging the War Office.

On the further side of this patch of land, which is a kind of isolated cape or shoulder in the hills, runs a very long, deep combe, which may be called Caterham Combe. Up this ran one of the Roman roads from the south, and up this runs to-day the modern road from Eastbourne to London. On the steep side of that precipitous ravine, which is a regular bank of difficult undergrowth (called Upwood Scrubbs), the Old Road was, as we had rightly expected from our previous study of the map, very hopelessly lost.

It is a difficult bit. Had the road followed round the outer side of the hill it would have been much easier to trace, but crossing as it does to the north of the summit, in order to avoid the re-entrant angle of Arthur's Seat, it has disappeared. For the damper soil upon that side, and the absence of a slope into which it could have cut its impression, has destroyed all evidence of the Old Road. One can follow it in the form of a rough lane up to the second of the War Office landmarks. After that it disappears altogether.

When one considers the condition of the terrain immediately to the east, the loss is not to be marvelled at. The hillside of Upwood Scrubbs falls very steeply into the valley by which the modern high-road climbs up to Caterham. It is an incline down which not even a primitive road would have attempted to go, and when one gets to the valley below the whole place is so cut up with the modern road, the old Roman road a little way to the east, and the remnants of a quarry just beyond, that it would have been impossible in this half-mile for the trace of the Pilgrim's Way to be properly preserved. I will, however, make this suggestion: that it descended the hillside diagonally going due NE. from the summit to the old gravel pit at the bottom, that then it curved round under the steep bank which supports Woodlands House, that is Dialbank Wood, went north of Quarry Cottage, and so reached the face of the hill again where the lane is struck which skirts round the southern edge of Marden Park. This, I say, will probably be found to be the exact track; but it is quite certain that the Way cannot have run more than a couple of hundred yards away from this curve. It cannot have been cut straight across the valley, for the steepness of the valley-side forbids that, and, on the other hand, there would have been no object in going much further up the valley than was necessary in order to save the steep descent.

At any rate, the gap is quite short and the road is easily recovered after the combe and the high-road are passed; it is thence identical with the lane I have spoken of above. This lane is called Flower Lane. It follows the -feet contour-line and winds therefore exactly round the outline of the hill. It passes the lodge of Marden Park, and within a few hundred yards comes to a place where the modern road bifurcates. The good macadamised lane goes straight on and somewhat downwards towards the plain. Another, less carefully made, begins to wind up the hill above one. From this point onward the Old Road takes again to the rough ground.

The Old Road

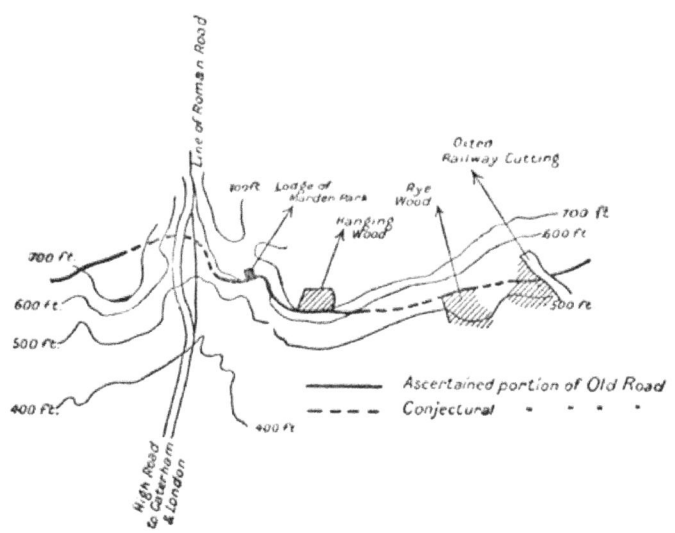

There lies just before one on the hillside a wood, called 'The Hanging Wood.'

We skirted the south edge of this wood and found beyond it a field in which the track is lost;[] nor was the task of recovering it an easy one, for the light was just failing, and here, as always where cultivation has risen above the old level, the Old Road is confused and destroyed.

We had, however, over these few yards an excellent clue. In a wood called 'The Rye Wood' just in front of us the track of the Old Road is not only clearly marked, but has been preserved by local traditions. For this NW. corner of the Rye Wood we made, through the south of the spinney called 'Hogtrough Spinney.'

Just beyond the Rye Wood, the hillside is pierced by a deep railway cutting which is the entrance to Oxted Tunnel. This cutting comes right across the line of the Old Road. We made for this point (which is a few yards north of the first bridge), but when we reached it, it was quite dark, and if we had covered in that day but eighteen miles or so, it must be remembered how much of our time had been spent in the perpetual checks of this division.[]

We reluctantly determined, then, to abandon the hillside for that evening, and to go down to the plain and sleep. The nearest place of hospitality was Oxted. We made for that village in the darkness, stumbling along the railway-line, and in the inn we met a third companion who had come to join us, and who would accompany us now as far as Canterbury.

When we had eaten and drunk wine, and had had some quarrelling with a chance traveller who suffered terribly from nerves, we left our entertainment. We slept, and the next morning, before it was light, we all three set out together, taking the northern road towards the hill.

Titsey to Wrotham
Sixteen miles

Beyond the railway-cutting, the road is recovered, as I have said, by tradition and by a constant use which lasted almost to our own time.[] It goes beneath the large wood which here clothes the hill, and after a partial loss in the field next the park, leads up to the farm known as 'Limpsfield Lodge Farm'; it comes to the paling of the park just north of the farm.

Across Titsey Park the track of the road is clear, and its interest is the greater from the anxiety which the owners of the place have shown to discover its antiquities.

A little off the Way, at the base of the hill, was discovered in a Roman villa, situated thus (as at Walton Heath, at Colley Hill, at Bletchingly, as later on at Burham, or, to take a remote instance, as in the case of the Roman village on the Evenlode, or again, that at Bignor) not right on the road itself, but from a quarter to half a mile off it. So the heirs of the Roman owners, the feudal lords, built their manor-houses off the roads and led to them by short perpendicular ways and avenues such as you may still see approaching half the French chateaux to-day.

It is probable (to guess at matters of which there is no proof) that while this road, serving no strategical purpose, leading to no frontier, and communicating between no two official centres of Roman life, was not used in the official system, the country people continued to make it one of their main ways, and that in the profound peace which the southern civilisation had imposed, the rich built for pleasure or to superintend their farms, along what was nothing but a British way.

Henceforward antiquities of every kind were to meet us as we advanced, because the Old Road on its way to the Straits gained importance with every ten miles of its way. Tributary roads continually fell into it: one had come in long ago at Alton, from Portsmouth and the Meon valley; at Farnham, a second had joined, which as the reader knows was probably older than the Old Road itself; others at the Guildford gap, others from the Weald and from the north as well at Dorking, another at Gatton, another at the Caterham Road: and each would swell the traffic and the movement upon this principal line of advance towards the Straits of Dover. More were to come. One of the highest importance (for it led from London along the valley of the Darent) was to join us at Otford; the last and perhaps the greatest, beyond the Medway, in the stretch before Boxley. With each of these the importance and the meaning of the road developed, and the increasing crowd of memories or records was like a company coming in on either side to press on with us to Canterbury.

Before leaving Titsey Park, the Old Road showed another of its characteristics in passing again just south of the site where the old church once stood; thenceforward for many miles it becomes a good modern lane, pursuing its way without deviation for five miles due east along the slope of the hills. Of this part, as of all such sections of our way, where a modern road coincides with the prehistoric way, there is little to be said. The level was not high, nor the vale immediately beneath us broad. Above us from the main ridge was granted, I knew by many journeys, that great vision: the whole southern plain, and above the near sand-hills, at one sweep, half the county of Sussex. But the matter of our journey forbade the enjoyment of such a sight, just as the matter of my book forbids me to speak of the very entertaining people of all kinds who came across us during these days and days, especially in the inns.

The road continues thus, following a contour between four and five hundred feet above sea-level, crosses the Kentish Border, and remains a good, well-kept lane, until it reaches the border of Chevening Park.

The right-of-way along the road across the park (where, of course, it has ceased to be a lane, and is no more than an indication upon the turf) has ceased since the passing of an Act of Parliament in the late eighteenth century, which Act diverts the traveller to the south, round the enclosure. But the direction taken by the Old Road across this ground is fairly evident until the last few hundred yards.

On the eastern side of the Park it is continued for about yards as a footpath. It is then lost under the plough; but a lane, some seven furlongs further on to the east, recovers the alignment,[] and leads straight on to the crossing of the Darent, down just such a spur as marked the crossing of the Mole, while above us went a flanking road, marked by stunted trees, on the windy edge of the Downs.

Following it thus we passed the northernmost of the two railway arches, went down the hill a mile or so, crossed the plain that was till recently marshy and difficult, and entered the village of Otford by the bridge and over the ford whereby, certainly since Edmund Ironside, and probably for many thousands of years before that, men had come to it.

Indeed, here, where the Old Road falls into the valley of the Darent, its importance in recorded history, which had been growing steadily as we went eastward, was suddenly increased for us, and the cause was the reception at this point of its tributary from London. From Otford the Old Road becomes strategic. It is the road by which marched the defending forces when invasion was threatened from the Thames estuary. It becomes hierarchic; the power of Canterbury seizes it; and it becomes royal, perpetually recalling the names and at last the tyranny of the kings. The battle against the invader, the king's progress to the sea, the hold of the Church upon the land it traverses, fill all the final marches from the crossing of the Darent to that of the Stour. Something of military history as at Alton, at Farnham, and just down the Stane Street at Anstie Bury, had attached even to the earlier part of so ancient a way—but from Otford onward it is greatly emphasised.

As one comes down from the chalk pit above the river one is crossing what is probably the site of Edmund Ironside's great and successful struggle with the Danes in , when he defeated Canute and drove him across the river, and pursued the rout mile upon mile to Aylesford. Half a mile further down on the plain, just before you get into the village, is the field where Offa is said to have achieved the supremacy of England by the conquest of Kent in .

It is only a doubtful bit of tradition, but it is worth recording that one more battle was fought here—as the populace believed—in the very first struggle of all—in the legendary fifth century. It is said that the Saxons were defeated here by the British, and that they also retreated towards Aylesford.

Canterbury had shown its influence long before this valley. We had seen the chapels and had but just left Brasted, whose allegiance to the archbishop was old beyond all record. But from Otford onward the power of the See became peculiar and more definite.

First there was the string of great palaces, Otford, Wrotham, Maidstone, Charing: Otford, Wrotham, and Charing especially, standing as they did directly upon the Old Road and created by it. We saw them all. They are in ruins.

Their authority, their meaning, had been suddenly destroyed. No one had claimed or supported their enormous walls. The new landlords of the Reformation, the swarm, the Cecils and the Russells and the rest, seem for once to have felt some breath of awe. The palaces were permitted to die. I imagined as I saw them one by one that the few stones remaining preserved a certain amplitude and magnificence; it may have been nothing but the fantasy of one who saw them thus for the first time, his mind already held for so many days by the antiquity of the Road.

They are forgotten. They were great for their time. Their life was intense. The economic power of the throne and of the chief altar in England ran through them. Otford at Domesday had its hundred small farms, its six mills; it was twice the size of Westerham. Wrotham and Charing, somewhat less, were yet (with Maidstone) the chief centres of Kent south of the Downs.

And apart from the See the Church in general held all the line. At Boxley, eldest daughter of Waverley, Clairvaux and the spirit of St. Bernard showed; it became as great as the palaces. Hollingbourne, fifty years before the Conquest, had been granted to St. Augustine's, a hundred years before that Lenham to Christchurch. The connection of Charing with Canterbury was so old that men believed their 'Vortigern' to have dedicated its land, and the church could show, even of writing, a parchment older than Alfred by a hundred years.

All these things had gone as utterly as the power to build and to think and to take joy in the ancient manner; the country-side we were treading held their principal and silent memorials.

For upon all this—which was England and the people—had fallen first the crown and then the rich, but the crown had begun the devastation.

I have said that from Otford the Old Road becomes royal, for it is at Otford that the road from Greenwich, after following the valley of the Darent, falls into the Pilgrim's Way. From Westminster by water to Greenwich, from Greenwich down here to Otford, and thence along the Old Road to the sea, had been a kind of sacred way, for the kings, who used as they went the great palaces of the Archbishops for their resting-places. By this road, last of so many, went Henry VIII. to the Field of the Cloth of Gold. It was an alternative to the straight road by Watling Street, and an alternative preferred from its age and dignity.

Then came its ruin. The grip of the crown caught up all the string of towns and villages and palaces and abbeys. You see the fatal date, 'th November, th Henry VIII.' recurring time and time again. Otford is seized, Wrotham is seized, Boxley, Hollingbourne, Lenham, Charing, and with these six great bases, a hundred detached and smaller things: barns, fields, mills, cells—all the way along this wonderful lane the memory of the catastrophe is scarred over the history of the country-side like the old mark of a wound, till you get to poor Canterbury itself and find it empty, with nothing but antiquarian guesses to tell you of what happened to the shrine and the bones of St. Thomas.

The Holy Well at Otford, its twin at Burham, the rood of Boxley, the block of Charing were trampled under. The common people, first apathetic, then troubled,—lastly bereft of religion, lost even the memory of the strong common life as the old men died; sites which had been sacred ever since men had put up the stones of Addington or Trottescliffe, or worshipped Mithra on the bank of the Medway, or put the three monoliths of Kit's Coty House together to commemorate their chief, or raised the hundred stones—all these were utterly forgotten.

It was not enough in this revolution that the Church should perish. The private lands of the most subservient were not safe—Kemsing, for example. It was the Manor of Anne Boleyn's father: it may be imagined what happened to such land. I know of no district in England where the heavy, gross, and tortured face of Henry in his decline haunts one more. Sacredness is twofold—of pleasure and pain—and this, the sacred end of our oldest travel, suffered in proportion to its sanctity.

When we had passed the Darent at Otford and climbed the hill beyond, we came upon a section of the road which might be taken as a kind of model of its character along these hills.

It is a section six miles long, beginning upon the hillside just above Otford station and ending near the schoolhouse above Wrotham. But in this short distance it gives examples of nearly all the points which it is the business of this book to describe. There is indeed no part of it here which requires to be sought out and mapped. The whole is known and has a continuous history; and such certitude is the more valuable in a typical division, because it permits us to deduce much that can elsewhere be applied to the less known portions of the road.

The Old Road runs here (as throughout nearly the whole of its course between Dorking and Canterbury) up on the bare hillside above the valley. The road appears, as one walks it, to run at the same level all along the hillside, but really it is rising as the floor of the valley rises, in order to keep continuously at the same distance above it. Its lowest point is not much under feet, but its highest is just over .

Immediately below it lies that string of habitations which everywhere marks its course, and between which it was originally the only means of communication. Just as Bletchingly, Reigate, Limpsfield, Westerham, Brasted, and the rest stood below its earlier course, and just as in its further part we shall find Hollingbourne, Harrietsham, Lenham and Charing, so here there runs a little succession of hamlets, churches, and small towns, which are the centres of groupings of arable land in the valley floor, while above them the Pilgrim's Road follows just above the margin of cultivation. Their names are Kemsing, Heaverham, St. Clere, Yaldham, and at last Wrotham.

The section further gives an admirable example of the way in which the Old Road was gradually replaced.

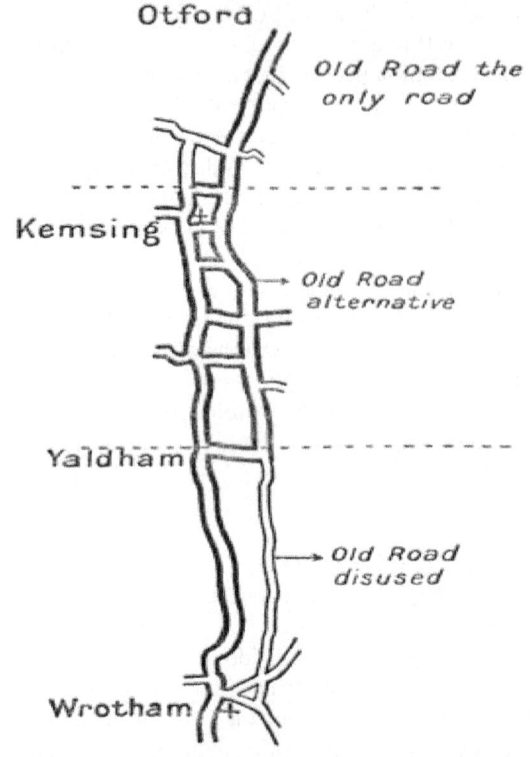

```
Otford
        Old Road the
        only road

Kemsing
        Old Road
        alternative

Yaldham
        Old Road
        disused

Wrotham
```

These six miles of its length may, for the purpose of the illustration they afford, be divided into three nearly equal parts by the village of Kemsing, and the hamlet of Yaldham. Each of these divisions shows the Old Road in one of its three historical phases: first as the only artery of the country-side, then as an alternative way supplemented by a valley road, and finally as a decayed and unused path whose value has been destroyed by the more modern highway below it. It is astonishing to see with what precision each of these phases is shown, how exactly each division ends, and how thoroughly the character of each is maintained.

In the first, from Otford to Kemsing, a distance of about two miles, one can see the two valley villages below one, and the track one follows is the only good road between them, though it lies above them both and can only be reached from either by a short rising lane. A short cut across the fields connects the two places, but if one wishes to use a proper and made way, there is none to take but that which still represents the Old Road, and so to go up out of Otford and then down into Kemsing. One has to do, in other words, exactly what was done for centuries when the archbishops came up to London from Canterbury; wherever one may desire to halt one has to leave the Old Road and come down from it to the village below.

In the second part, between Kemsing and Yaldham, the modern influence has been sufficient to provide an alternative. The distance is somewhat more than two miles. The Pilgrim's Way runs up along the hillside, a metalled lane, while below in the valley the old footpaths and cart tracks have been united into a modern permanent road, and a man going from Kemsing through Heaverham to Yaldham need not take the Pilgrim's Road above as his ancestors would have had to do, but can go straight along the lower levels.

Finally, with Yaldham and on to Wrotham the more common condition of modern times asserts itself. The lower valley road becomes the only important one, the Pilgrim's Road above dwindles into, first, a lane very little used and falling into decay, then a path thick with brambles and almost impassable. A man going from Yaldham to Wrotham nowadays is bound to use the modern valley road. When we had pushed through the brambles of the deserted path for perhaps a mile and a half, the way broadened out again, crossed the London Road, and turning the corner of the hill overlooked the church and roofs of Wrotham a hundred feet below.

Of Wrotham, the second link in that chain of palaces which afforded shelter to the Archbishop and to the King, as the one journeyed to Lambeth, the other to the sea-coast, I have already spoken. I desire here to discuss rather the topographical interest of the corner upon which we stood and its connection with the prehistoric road which it was our principal business to examine.

And for that purpose, though it occupied but the last part of a day, I would devote to a separate division the passage of the Medway which was now at hand.

Wrotham to Boxley
Eleven miles
At Wrotham is a kind of platform, or rather shoulder, which is made by such a turning of the great chalk hills as I shall presently describe. This turning revealed to us the plain at our feet as we came round the corner of the hill and saw before us the whole valley of the Medway.

We were perhaps some hundred feet above Wrotham and five hundred above the sea as we stood upon this platform before noon, and overlooked the great flats and the distant river and the further hills.

It is a view of astonishing effect, such as I did not know to be in south England; for our rivers are small, and, exquisite as is their scenery, they do not commonly impress the mind with grandeur. The Medway, perhaps because it is the relic of some much greater river now drowned by the sinking of the land, perhaps because its tidal estuary lends it twice a day an artificial breadth, gives one the impression of those continental streams, the Seine or the Meuse, which are sufficient to animate a whole country-side, and which run in so wide a basin that a whole province attaches to their name.

The manner of this landscape was that of a great gesture; its outline was like the movement of a hand that sketches a cartoon; its sweep was like the free arm of a sower sowing broadcast. The bank, moreover, upon which the Old Road here stands is so steep that it produces an effect of greater height and whatever expansion of the mind accompanies a wide horizon.

There dominated that view a character of space and dignity which not even the Itchen valley from the heights, nor the Weald from the crest of the Surrey Downs, could equal. The crossings of the Wey, of the Mole, and of the Darent, the valleys which there interrupted the general line of our hillside road, seemed narrow and familiar as one gazed upon this much greater plain.

Far off, miles and miles away, the hills continued their interminable line. The haze, and a certain warm quality in the winter light, added to the vastness of the air, and made the distant range seem as remote as a to-morrow; it was lost in a grey-blue that faded at last into a mere sky upon the extreme east.

Along those hills our way was clearly to be continued. Their trend was not, indeed, due east and west as the Old Road had run so long: they turned a little southerly; but the general line, bending down to Canterbury and to the Straits, followed that crest, and its furthest visible height was not far distant from our goal.

Just opposite us, upon the further side of the valley, was faintly to be discerned such another shoulder as that upon which we stood. We made it out upon our map to bear the good name of 'Grey Wethers,' as does that rock far off eastwards, out of which was built Stonehenge. Upon that shoulder had stood the abbey of Boxley. It marked the point where, beyond the valley, the Pilgrim's Way is recognised again. But in the interval between, across this broad flat valley, its passage had never been fixed.

We might have thought, had we not hitherto learnt much of the Old Road, that no problem was there, save to cross in a direct line the valley before us, and make by evening that further shoulder of 'Grey Wethers,' where we should find the road again; but we had followed the track too long to think that it could so easily be recovered. We guessed that in so wide a gap as was here made by the Medway in the line of hills a difficulty, greater than any we had yet met, would arise, and that we should not overcome it without a longer search than had been necessary at the Wey or even the Mole.

We were now familiar with such platforms and such views. Upon a lesser scale we had felt their meaning when we stood upon the rock of St. Catherine's at evening and considered the crossing of the Wey; or on that other spur, eastward of Dorking, when we had seen Box Hill beyond the valley under the growing night. They also, the men long before us, had chosen such particular places from whence to catch the whole of a day's march, and to estimate their best opportunity for getting to the further shore.

We knew how difficult it was to trace again their conclusion, and to map out the Old Road in places like these.

To debate its chances and draw up the main line of our decision, we went down into Little Wrotham, and at an inn there which is called the 'Bull,' we ate beef and drank beer, spoke with men who knew the fords and the ferries, compared our maps with a much older one belonging to the place, and in general occupied our minds with nothing but the passage of the river: the passage, that is, which alone concerned us; the place where men, when men first hunted here, fixed their crossing-place, and carried the Old Road across the tide-way of the stream.

Now, having said so much of the landscape, it is necessary to turn to the more minute task of topography. For it is the business of this book not to linger upon the pleasures of our journey, but to reconstitute an ancient thing. And for that purpose a simple sketch-map will explain perhaps as much as words can do.

The features of this map are very few, but their comprehension will be sufficient for my readers to grasp the matter upon which we are engaged.

A single heavy line indicates the crest of the hills—a crest from over six hundred to over seven hundred feet in height. A dotted line indicates the limit of what may be called the floor of the valley. The brackets)(show the four possible crossings of the river. Two points, numbered *A* and *B*, mark the 'shoulders' or platform. The first (*A*) above Wrotham, the second (*B*) at Grey Wethers. Finally, the megalithic monument at Coldrum and that near Grey Wethers (whose importance will be seen in a moment) are marked with circles.

Far up the valley on each hill continues the remnant of an ancient road, and the reader will see from this, that, as in the valley of the Mole and of the Darent, our difficulties were confused and increased from the fact that, quite apart from the crossing of the river, other prehistoric tracks led off northwards upon either side of the river, whose crossing was our concern.

The great main range of chalk which runs all across south-eastern England; the range whose escarpment affords for sixty miles a platform for the Old Road is broken, then, by the Medway, which cuts through it on its way to the sea. But there is not only a gap; it will be seen that the hills 'bend up,' as it were, upon either bank, and follow the stream northward, making a kind of funnel to receive it. The effect of this is best expressed by saying, that it is as though the Medway valley had been scooped out by a huge plough, which not only cut a five-mile gap in the range, but threw the detritus of such a cutting to left and right for miles beyond the point of its passage. It is at the mouth of this gap that the two shoulders or turning-places are to be found; one on the west at Wrotham, the other on the east at Grey Wethers: while beyond them the Downs turn northward either way, to sink at last into the flats of the Thames estuary.

The interval between these 'shoulders' was the most considerable of any that had to be filled in all our exploration.

The reason that this gap in the Old Road should be found at such a place was evident. It was here that the road had to cross the most important of the rivers it meets upon its course, the Medway. Alone of the rivers which obstruct the road, it is a tidal stream, and, as though in recognition of its superior claim, the hills receded from it more grandly than they had from the Wey at the Guildford, or the Mole at the Dorking passage. They left six miles of doubtful valley between them, and across these six miles a track had to be found.

THE MOST IMPORTANT OF THE RIVERS IT MEETS UPON ITS COURSE, THE MEDWAY

A clear statement of the problem will lead one towards its solution.

I have said that for several miles before Wrotham, the chalk hills, well defined and steep, running almost due east and west, present an excellent dry and sunny bank for the road. As one goes along this part of one's journey, Wrotham Hill appears like a kind of cape before one, because beyond it the hills turn round northward, and their continuation is hidden. I have also told how, a long way off, over the broad flat of the Medway valley, the range may be seen continuing in the direction of Canterbury, and affording, when once the river is crossed, a similar platform to that from which one is gazing.

We knew, also, that the road does, as a fact, follow those distant hills, precisely as it had the range from which we made our observation, and if no physical obstacles intervened, the first travellers upon this track would undoubtedly have made a direct line from the projecting shoulder of Wrotham Hill to the somewhat less conspicuous turning-point which marks the further hills of Grey Wethers, where also Boxley once stood.

But obstacles do intervene, and these obstacles were of the most serious kind for men who had not yet passed the early stages of civilisation. A broad river with a swift tidal current, flanked here and there (as tidal rivers always are before their embankment) by marshes; a valley floor of clay, the crossing of which must prove far more lengthy than that of any they had hitherto encountered, made the negotiation of this gap a difficult matter. Moreover, the direct line would have led them by the marshiest way of all: the fields of Snodland brook.

Oddly enough the difficulty of rediscovering the original track by which the road forded the Medway, does not lie in the paucity of evidence, but rather in the confusion arising from its nature and amount. So great is this confusion that some authorities have been content to accept alternative routes at this point.

Savage trails, however, never present alternatives so widely separate, and least of all will they present any alternative, even one neighbouring the main road, where a formidable obstacle has to be overcome: to do so would be to forfeit the whole value which a primitive road possesses as a guide (for this value depends upon custom and memory), and when a tidal river had to be traversed, a further and very cogent reason for a single track was to be found in the labour which its construction upon a marshy soil involved.

If some one place of crossing had held a monopoly or even a pre-eminence within the limits of recorded history, the evidence afforded by it would be of the utmost value. But an indication of this simplicity is lacking.

It is certain that within historic times and for many centuries continuously, the valley and the river were passed at four places, each of which now may lay a claim to be the original passage.

The modern names of these places are, in their order from the sea, Cuxton, Lower Halling, Snodland, and Aylesford.

Before proceeding I must repeat what was said above, that two tracks of great antiquity continue the Old Road northward on each side of the Medway far beyond any point where it would have crossed; these tracks (I have called them elsewhere 'feeders') are not only clearly defined, but have each received the traditional name of the Pilgrim's Way, and their presence adds a considerable complexity to the search for the original passage.

So much of the elements of the problem being laid down, let us now recapitulate certain features which we have discovered to be true of the road in the earlier part of its course, where it had to cross a river, and certain other features which one knows to be common to other British track-ways over valleys broader than those of the Mole or the Wey. To these features we may add a few others, which are conjecturally those that such a road would possess although we might have no direct evidence of them.

A list of these features will run very much as follows:—

() The road will attempt the shortest passage of the valley floor, the breadth being more or less of an obstacle, according as the soil is more or less low, covered, or damp.

() It will seek for a ford.

() Other things being equal, it would naturally cross a river as high up as possible, where the stream was likely to be less difficult to ford.

() It would cross in as immediate a neighbourhood as possible to that height upon which survey could be made of the opportunities for crossing.

() The nature of the bottom at the crossing would influence it greatly, whether that bottom were gravel and sand, or treacherous mud. Moreover, a primitive road would often leave evidence of its choice by the relics of good material thrown in to harden the ford.

() A point of so much importance would probably be connected with religion, and almost always with some relic of habitation or weapons.

() It would often preserve in its place-name some record of the crossing.

() It would (as we had found it at Dorking and at Otford) choose a place where a spur on either side led down to the river.

To these eight points may be added the further consideration, that whatever was the more usual crossing in early historic times affords something of a guide as to prehistoric habits, and, finally, that where a tidal river was concerned, the motives which were present on any river for seeking a passage as far up stream as possible would be greatly strengthened, for the tide drowns a ford.

Now, in the light of what the map tells us, and of these principles, let us see where the crossing is most likely to be found, and having determined that, discover how far the hypothesis is supported by other evidence.

To begin with Cuxton:

At Cuxton the firm land of the hills comes upon either side close to the river. An ancient track-way upon either side leads very near to the point of crossing and cannot be followed, or at least nothing like so clearly followed further down the valley. At Cuxton, moreover, as a constant tradition maintains, the crossing of the river by pilgrims was common.

On the other hand there is nothing approaching a ford at this place. The bottom is soft mud, the width of the river very considerable, the tidal current strong, and of all the points at which the river might have been crossed, it is the most distant from the direct line; indeed, compared with the next point, Lower Halling, a traveller would add five or six miles to his journey by choosing Cuxton.

Now, consider Aylesford, the other extreme; the highest up as Cuxton is the lowest down the river of the four points. Aylesford has many powerful arguments in its favour. It has produced one of the most interesting and suggestive prehistoric relics in England: I mean that 'Aylesford pottery' which is an imitation, or possibly even an import, of the pottery of northern Italy in the first or second centuries before our area. It has furnished a mass of other antiquities: armillae of gold have been found in the river and British coins and graves on the northern bank. It preserves in the last part of its name the tradition of a ford, and though 'ford' in place-names by no means always signifies a ford any more than 'bridge' signifies a bridge, yet in this case we have historic knowledge that a ford existed; and (as is most frequently the case) the ford has been bridged.

A further argument, and in its way one of the strongest that could be adduced, is the position of the place in the earliest of our annals. Whether 'the Horse and the Mare,' Vortigern, and the rest are wholly legendary or not, cannot be determined. Certainly the texture of the story is fabulous, but Bede and 'Nennius' have both retained the memory of a great battle fought here, in which the British overcame the Pirates, and what is most significant of all, the legend or memory records a previous retreat of the Saxons from a defeat at Otford. We know, therefore, that a writer in the seventh century, though what he was writing might be fable, would take it for granted that a retreat westward from Otford would naturally lead along some road which passed the Medway at Aylesford. We get another much later example of the same thing when Edmund Ironside, after his great victory at Otford over the Danes, pursued them to Aylesford, and was only prevented from destroying them by their passage over the river under the cover of treason.

This is very strong evidence in favour of Aylesford, and when one remembers that the manor was ancient demesne, its antiquity and importance are enhanced.

But against Aylesford there are three strong arguments. They are not only strong, they are insuperable. The first is the immense width of valley that would have to be crossed to reach it. That is, the immense tract of uncertain, wooded way, without a view either of enemies or of direction.

The second is the clay. A belt of gault of greater or lesser width stretches all along the Downs just below the chalk. Here it is particularly wide, and no straight line can be taken from Wrotham to the Aylesford gravels without crossing nearly two miles of this wretched footing, which, throughout its course, the road has most carefully avoided. That a ford of great antiquity was there; that the men of the sandy heights used it; that the Romans used so admirable a ford (it is gravel near the river on either side), that they bridged it, that they made a causeway over the clay, and that this causeway and that bridge were continuously used after their time, I am willing to believe; but not that the prehistoric road along the chalk hills could have waded through all that clay to reach it, and have gone out of its way into the bargain.

Thirdly, there is the clinching fact that a number of prehistoric remains, Kit's Coty House and the rest, lie to the *north* of such a crossing, and that to reach Boxley itself, a site indubitably dependent upon the prehistoric road, a man crossing at Aylesford would have to turn *back* upon his general direction.

It must further be remembered that by the seventh century some of the valleys had acquired firm roads, inherited from the old civilisation, and that in the rout after a battle, an army making for a tidal river, and not able to choose their own time of crossing (as can a wayfarer), would certainly make for a point as far up the stream as possible and for a bridge.

If Cuxton and Aylesford, then, are to be neglected (as I think they certainly must be), there remain only Lower Hailing and Snodland.

At first sight the weight of argument is for Lower Halling, and if the various parts of such an argument as I adduce have different proportions from those I lend them, one might conclude that at Lower Halling was the original passage of the Medway.

True, there is for the passage at Lower Halling but one evidence that I can discover, but it is an evidence of the greatest weight, and such an one as is often permitted alone to establish a conclusion in archæology. It is this, that there was good surface over the original soil from the Pilgrim's Way on the hills above, right down to the river-bank at this point. No clay intervenes between the chalk and gravel. The primitive traveller would have had fairly dry land all the way down to the river. Even beyond the river the belt of alluvial soil is less broad than it is at Snodland; and altogether, if the geological argument alone were considered, the decision undoubtedly would be given to this place.

The claims of Snodland are asserted by a number of converging arguments. I will enumerate them, and it will, I think, be seen that though each is individually slight, the whole bundle is convincing.

First.—The spur, which leaves the main range of hills for the river (such a spur as has elsewhere, at Shalford, and at Dorking, and at Otford, attracted the Old Road towards the ford it points to), touches indeed both Snodland and Lower Halling on either side, but with this great difference—that Snodland is on the south, Lower Halling upon the north of the ridge. The elevation is not pronounced, the slope is slight, but a little experience of such ground at various seasons will determine one that the southern bank would be chosen under primitive conditions. In such a conformation the southern bank alone has during the winter any chance of drying, and in a dry summer, it matters little whether a slope be partly of clay[] (as is the descent to Snodland) or of chalk (as is that to Lower Halling). During more than half the year, therefore, the descent to Snodland was preferable; during the other half indifferent.

Secondly.—Immediately before and beyond the Lower Halling crossing no antiquities of moment have been discovered: a grave, possibly Roman, is, I believe, the only one. At Snodland, and beyond its crossing, they are numerous. An ancient and ruined chapel marks the descent from the hills. The church itself has Roman tiles. Beyond the river, the Roman villa which was unearthed in by Mr. Patrick is precisely upon the road that would lead from such a crossing up to the Pilgrim's Way upon the hill. Close by the origin of this lane from the ford to the hillside were discovered the fragments of what some have believed to be a Mithraic temple; and earlier, in , Roman urns and foundations were found near the road at Little Culand.

Thirdly.—The crossing at Snodland is shallower than that at Lower Halling, and (though I do not pretend that the artifice is prehistoric) the bottom has been artificially hardened.

Fourthly.—There stands at Snodland a church, past the *southern* porch of which goes the road, and when the river is crossed, and the same alignment followed along the bank upon the further side for a little way, the track again passes by a church, and again by its *southern* porch.

Fifthly.—The 'Horseshoe Reach'—the reach, that is, between Snodland and Burham—has always marked the limit between Rochester's jurisdiction over the lower, and Maidstone's over the upper, Medway. This is of great importance. All our tidal rivers have a sea-town and a land-town; the limits up to which the seaport has control is nearly always the *traditional crossing-place* of the river. Thus Yarmouth Stone on the Yare divides the jurisdiction of Norwich from that of Yarmouth; it is close to the Reedham Ferry, which has always been the first passage over the river. For London and the Thames we have the best example of all—Staines.

Finally, it is not extravagant to note how the megalithic monument (now fallen) near Trottescliffe, corresponds to Kit's Coty House on the opposite shoulder beyond the valley. The crossing at Snodland would be the natural road between the two.

ROCHESTER

These seven converging lines of proof, or rather of suggestion—seven points which ingenuity or research might easily develop into a greater number—seem to me to settle the discussion in favour of Snodland.[]

By that ferry then we crossed. We noted the muddy river, suggestive of the sea, the Medway, which so few miles above suggests, when it brims at high tide, a great inland river. It has hidden reaches whose fields and trees have quite forgotten the sea. We passed by the old church at Burham. We were in a very field of antiquity[] as we went our way, and apart from the stones and fragments it has left, we were surrounded by that great legend which made this place the funeral of the first barbarians.

It was already nearly dark when we came to the place where that old sphinx of three poised monoliths, Kit's Coty House, stands in a field just north of the lane; the old circle of stones, now overthrown, lay below us to the south.

We would not pass Kit's Coty House without going near it to touch it, and to look at it curiously with our own eyes. Though we were very weary, and though it was now all but dark, we trudged over the plough to where it stood; the overwhelming age of the way we had come was gathered up in that hackneyed place.

Whether the name be, or be not, a relic of some Gaelic phrase that should mean 'the grave in the wood,' no one can tell. The wood has at any rate receded, and only covers in patches the height of the hill above; but that repeated suggestion of the immense antiquity of the trail we were pursuing came to us from it again as we hesitated near it, filled us with a permanent interest, and for a moment overcame our fatigue.

When we had struck the high-road some yards beyond, just at the place where the Pilgrims Way leaves it to reach the site where Boxley Abbey once stood, our weakness returned. Not that the distance we had traversed was very great, but that this kind of walking, interrupted by doubts and careful search, and much of it of necessity taken over rough land, had exhausted us more than we knew.

With difficulty, though it was by a fine, great falling road, we made the town of Maidstone, and having dined there in the principal inn to the accompaniment of wine, we determined to complete the journey, if possible, in the course of the next day.

Boxley to Canterbury
Twenty-six miles
From Boxley to Charing the Old Road presents little for comment, save that over these thirteen miles it is more direct, more conspicuously marked, and on the whole better preserved than in any other similar stretch of its whole course. The section might indeed be taken as a type of what the primitive wayfarers intended when the conditions offered them for their journey were such as they would have chosen out of all. It is not a permanent road as is the section between Alton and Farnham, therefore nothing of its ancient character is obliterated. On the other hand, it is not—save in two very short spaces— interfered with by cultivation or by private enclosure. This stretch of the road is a model to scale, preserved, as though by artifice, from modern changes, and even from decay, but exhibiting those examples of disuse which are characteristic of its history.

The road goes parallel to and above the line where the sharp spring of the hill leaves the floor of the valley; it commands a sufficient view of what is below and of what lies before; it is well on the chalk, just too high to interfere with cultivation, at least with the cultivation of those lower levels to which the Middle Ages confined themselves; it is well dried by an exposure only a little west of south; it is well drained by the slope and by the porous soil; it is uninterrupted by combes, or any jutting promontories, for the range of the hills is here exactly even. In a word, it here possesses every character which may be regarded as normal to the original trail from the west of England to the Straits of Dover.

The villages which lie immediately below it are all at much the same distance—from a quarter to half a mile: it can be said to traverse one alone— Detling, and this it passes through to the north. The others, Harrietsham, Hollingbourne, Lenham, Charing, are left just to the south. They are now connected by the high-road which joins up the valley, and were once, it may be presumed, isolated from each other by the common fields and the waste of each village, or if connected, connected only by paths. They may have depended, during many centuries, for their intercommunication, upon the Old Road, to which each of them possesses a definitely marked line of approach: and the Old Road remains the typical main artery, which passes near, but not through, the places it serves.[]

This thirteen miles of the way is often vague, and is indeed actually broken at one point between Cobham Farm and Hart Hill, a mile and a half east of Charing; but it is a gap which presents no difficulty. The alignment is precisely the same before and after it; it is but seven furlongs in extent; it has been caused by the comparatively recent ploughing of this land during the two generations of our history when food was dear.

From Boxley to Lenham the plain beneath the Old Road is drained by a stream called the Len, tributary to the Medway. Just before or at Lenham is the watershed: a parting of no moment, not a ridge, hardly observable to one standing above it on the hillside. It is the dividing line between the basins of the Medway and the Stour. All the hydrography of south-eastern England presents this peculiarity. The watersheds are low; the bold ranges do not divide the river-basins, because the water system is geologically older than the Chalk Hills.

The Stour rises in Lenham itself, but its course has at first no effect upon the landscape, so even is the plain below. A village, which preserves the great Norman name of the Malherbes, stands on the watershed: the whole flat saddle is a rich field diversified by nothing more than slight rolls of land, in between which the spring comes as though up from a warmer earth, long before it touches the hills.

It is peculiar in England, this county of Kent, and especially its valleys. I had known it hitherto only as a child, a stranger, but no one who has so visited it in childhood can forget the sheep in the narrow lanes, or the leaning cones of the hop-kilns against the sky: the ploughlands under orchards: all the Kentish Weald.

At Charing the great hills begin to turn a corner. The Stour also turns, passes through a wide gap, and from east and south begins to make north and east straight for Canterbury; henceforward the spirit of Canterbury and the approach to it occupies the road.

We had reached the end of that long, clean-cut ridge which we had followed all the way from Farnham, the ridge which the four rivers had pierced in such well-defined gaps. Charing is the close of that principal episode in the life of the Way.

THE SHEEP IN THE NARROW LANES, OR THE LEANING CONES OF THE HOP-KILNS AGAINST THE SKY

Charing again was the last convenient halt in any rich man's journey until, say, a hundred and fifty years ago. It is something under sixteen miles from Canterbury, following the track of the Old Road, and even the poor upon their pilgrimages would have halted there; though the slow progress of their cumbersome caravans may have forced them to a further repose at Chilham before the city was reached.

Charing, therefore, was designed by its every character to be a place of some importance, and was a very conscious little town.

It counts more in Domesday than any other of the valley villages between Maidstone and the cathedral; it possessed the greatest and the first of those archiepiscopal palaces, the string of which we came on first at Otford; it has a church once magnificent and still remarkable after its rebuilding, and it maintains to this day an air of prosperity and continued comfort. The inn is one of the best inns to be found on all this journey; the whole village may be said, in spite of its enemies,[] to be livelier in the modern decay than the other remote parishes of that plain.

We had imagined, before seeing the ground, that, after Charing, we should have some difficulty in tracing the Old Road.

The Ordnance map, which has given it the traditional name of the Pilgrim's Road all through this valley, not only drops the title immediately after Charing, but, for some reason I do not understand, omits to mark it at all along the skirts of Longbeech wood.

When we came to follow it up, however, we found it a plainly-marked lane, leading at much the same height round the shoulder of the hill, to the western lodge of Lord Gerrard's park. Just before we entered that park two local names emphasised the memories of the road: the cottage called 'Chapel' and the word 'Street' in 'Dun Street' at the lodge.

Within the fence of this park it is included. For nearly a mile the fence of the park itself runs on the embankment of the Old Road. At the end of that stretch, the fence turns a sharp angle outwards, and for the next mile and a half, the road, which is here worn into the clearest of trenches and banks, goes right across the park till it comes out on the eastern side a few yards to the south of the main gates. The Old Road thus turns a gradual corner, following the curve of the Stour valley.

The modern road from Charing to Canterbury cuts off this corner, and saves a good two miles or three, but the reasons which caused men in the original condition of the country to take the longer course of the Old Road are not far to seek.

There is, first, that motive which we have seen to be universal, the dryness of the road, which could only be maintained upon the southern side of the hill.

Next, it must be noted that these slopes down to the Stour were open when the plateau above was dense forest. This in its turn would mean a group of villages—such a group is lacking even to this day to the main road, and the way would naturally follow where the villages lay.

Finally, the water-supply of the plateau was stagnant and bad; that of the valley was a good running stream.

In its passage through Eastwell Park, the road passed near the site of the house, and it passed well north of the church, much as it had passed north of the parishes in the valley we had just left. This would lead one to conjecture, I know not with what basis of probability, that a village once existed near the water around the church at the bottom of the hill. If it did, no trace of it now remains, but whether (already in decay) it was finally destroyed, as some have been by enclosure, or whether the church, being the rallying-point of a few scattered farmhouses (as is more often the case), was enclosed without protest and without hurt to its congregation, I have no means of determining. It is worth noting, that no part of the Old Road is enclosed for so great a length as that which passes from the western to the eastern lodge of Eastwell Park. Nearly two miles of its course lies here within the fence of a private owner.

It is odd to see how little of the road has fallen within private walls. In Hampshire nothing of it is enclosed; in Surrey, if we except the few yards at Puttenham, and the garden rather than the park at Monk's Hatch, it has been caught by the enclosures of the great landlords in four places alone: Albury, Denbies, Gatton, and Titsey. It passes, indeed, through the gardens of Merstham House, but that only for a very short distance.

In Kent, Chevening has absorbed it for now close upon a century; then it remains open land as far as this great park of Eastwell, and, as we shall see, passes later through a portion of Chilham.

Clear as the road had been throughout Eastwell Park (and preserved possibly by its enclosure), beyond the eastern wall it entirely disappears. The recovery of it, rather more than half a mile further on, the fact that one recovers it on the same contour-line, that the contour-line is here turned round the shoulder of the hill which forms the entrance into the valley of the Stour, give one a practical certainty that the Old Road swept round a similar curve, but the evidence is lost.[]

The portion near Boughton Aluph is perfectly clear; it goes right up under the south porch. It has disappeared again under the plough in the field between the church and Whitehill Farm. There it has been cut, as we had found it so often in the course of our journey, by a quarry. Another field has lost it again under the plough; it reappears on the hillside beyond in a line of yews.[] But within a hundred yards or so there arises a difficulty which gave rise to some discussion among us.

A little eastward of us, on the way we had to go, the range of hills throws out one of those spurs with a re-entrant curve upon the far side, which we had previously discovered in Surrey above Red Hill and Bletchingly. It was our experience that the Old Road, when it came to an obstacle of this kind, made for the neck of the promontory and cut off the detour by passing just north of the crest. The accompanying sketch will explain the matter.

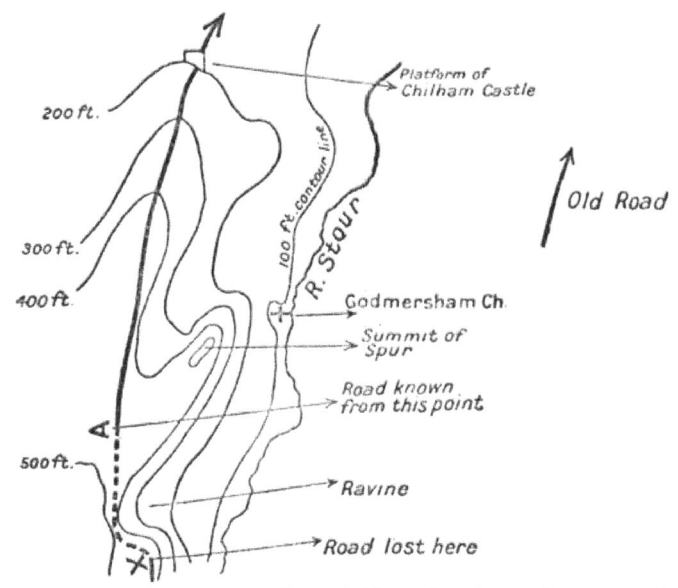

Sketch map labels: 200 ft., 300 ft., 400 ft., 500 ft.; Platform of Chilham Castle; 100 ft. contour line; R. Stour; Godmersham Ch.; Summit of Spur; Road known from this point; Ravine; Road lost here; Old Road; X; A.

We knew from the researches of others that the road was certainly to be found again at the spot marked A. It was our impression, from a previous study of the map, that the trail would make straight for this point from the place where I was standing (X). But we were wrong. At this point the road turned *up* the hill, its track very deeply marked, lined with trees, and at the top with yews of immense antiquity. The cause of this diversion was apparent when we saw that the straight line I had expected the road to follow would have taken it across a ravine too shallow for the contours of the Ordnance map to indicate, but too steep for even a primitive trail to have negotiated. And this led me to regret that we had not maps of England such as they have for parts of Germany, Switzerland, and France, which give three contour-lines to every feet, or one to every metres.

We followed up the hill, then, certain that we had recovered the Old Road. It took the crest of the hill, went across the open field of Soakham, plunged into a wood, and soon led us to the point marked upon my sketch as A, where any research of ours was no longer needed. It is from this place that a man after all these hundred miles can first see Canterbury.

We looked through the mist, down the hollow glen towards the valley between walls of trees. We thought, perhaps, that a dim mark in the haze far off was the tower of the Cathedral—we could not be sure. The woods were all round us save on this open downward upon which we gazed, and below us in its plain the discreet little river the Stour. The Way did not take us down to that plain, but kept us on the heights above, with the wood to our left, and to our right the palings of Godmersham.

THE PLOUGHLANDS UNDER ORCHARDS: ALL THE KENTISH WEALD

We had already learnt, miles westward of this, that the Old Road does not take to the crest of a hill without some good reason, but that once there it often remains, especially if there is a spur upon which it can fall gently down to the lower levels.

The lane we were following observed such a rule. It ran along the north of Godmersham Park, just following the highest point of the hill, and I wondered whether here, as in so many other places, it had not formed a natural boundary for the division of land; but I have had no opportunity of examining the history of this enclosure. Chilham Park marches with Godmersham; where one ends and the other begins the road passed through the palings (and we with it) and went on in the shape of a clear ridge, planted often with trees, right down to the mound on which stands Chilham Castle.

Down in the valley below, something much older bore witness to the vast age of this corner of inhabited land: the first barrow to be opened in England; the tomb in which Camden (whom Heaven forgive) thought that a Roman soldier lay; in which the country people still believe that the great giant Julaber was buried, but which is the memorial of something far too old to have a name.

This castle and this grave are the entry into that host of antiquities which surrounds upon every side the soil of Canterbury. In every point of the views which would strike us in the last few miles, the history of this island would be apparent.

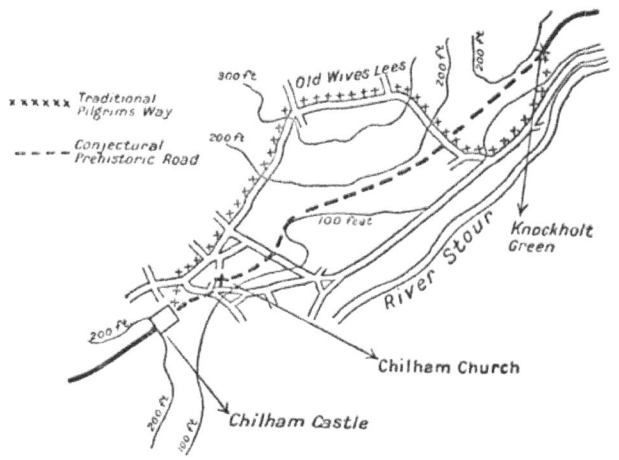

From the mound on which Chilham Castle stands to the farm called Knockholt, just two miles away, is what I believe to be a gap in the Old Road, and I will give my reasons for that conviction. Did I not hold it, my task would be far easier, for all the maps give the Way continuously from point to point.

Up to the mound of Chilham the path is clear. After Knockholt it is equally clear, and has, for that matter, been studied and mapped by the highest authority in England.[] But to bridge the space between is not as easy as some writers would imagine.

It will be apparent from this sketch-map that between Chilham and Knockholt there rises a hill. On the south-east of it flows the Stour, with the modern main road alongside of it; on the north two lanes, coming to an angle, lead through a hamlet called Old Wives' Lees.

There is a tradition that the pilgrims of the later Middle Ages went through Chilham and then turned back along these northern lanes, passing through Old Wives' Lees. This tradition may be trusted. They may have had some special reason, probably some devotional reason, for thus going out of their way, as we found them to have had at Compton. If their action in this is a good guide (as their action usually is) to the trace of the Old Road, well and good; there is then no appreciable gap, for a path leads to Knockholt and could only correspond to the Old Road; but I should imagine that here, as at Merstham, the pilgrims may have deceived us. They may have made a detour for the purpose of visiting some special shrine, or for some other reason which is now forgotten. It is difficult to believe that a prehistoric trail would turn such sharp corners, for the only time in all this hundred and twenty miles, without some obvious reason, and that it should choose for the place in which to perform this evolution the damp and northern side of a rather loamy hill. I cannot but believe that the track went over the side of the hill upon the southern side, but I will confess that if it did so there is here the longest and almost the only unbridged gap in the whole of the itinerary. I am confirmed in my belief that it went over the southern side from the general alignment, from the fact that the known path before Chilham goes to the south of the castle mound, that this would lead one to the south of the church, and so over the southern shoulder of the hill; but, if it did so, ploughed land and the careful culture of hop-gardens have destroyed all traces of it. I fancied that something could be made of an indication about a quarter of a mile before Knockholt Farm, but I doubt whether it was really worth the trouble of examining.[]

From the farm, right up through Bigberry Wood, we were on a track not only easy to recognise, but already followed, as I have said, by the first of authorities upon the subject.

We came after a mile of the wood to the old earthwork which was at once the last and the greatest of the prehistoric remains upon the Old Road, and the first to be connected with written history.

It was a good place to halt: to sit on the edge of the gravelly bank, which had been cast up there no one knows how many centuries ago, and to look eastward out towards Canterbury.

The fort was not touched with the memory of the Middle Ages: it was not our goal, for that was the church of St. Thomas, but it was the most certain and ancient thing of all that antiquity which had been the meaning of the road, and it stood here on the last crest of so many heights from which we had seen so many valleys in these eight days.

History and the prehistoric met at this point only.

Elsewhere we had found very much of what men had done before they began to write down their deeds. We had passed the barrows and the entrenchments, and the pits from whence coins with names, but without a history or a date, had been dug, and we had trodden on hard ground laid down at fords by men who had left no memory. We had seen also a very great many battlefields of which record exists. We had marched where Sweyn marched; Cheriton had been but a little way upon our right; we had seen Alton; the Roman station near Farnham had stood above us; the great rout of Ockley had lain not far off below our passage of the Mole; and we had recalled the double or treble memory of Otford, and of the Medway valley, where the invader perpetually met the armies of the island.

But in all these there were two clean divisions: either the thing was archaic—a subject for mere guess-work; or it was clear history, with no prehistoric base that we knew of behind it.

On this hill the two categories mingled, and a bridge was thrown between them. For it was here that the Roman first conquered. This was that defence which the Tenth Legion stormed: the entrenchment which was the refuge for Canterbury; and the river which names the battle was that dignified little stream the Stour, rolling an even tide below.

The common people, who have been thought to be vacant of history, or at the best to distort it, have preserved a memory of this fight for two thousand years.

I remembered as I sat there how a boy, a half-wit, had told me on a pass in Cumberland that a great battle had been fought there between two kings; he did not know how long ago, but it had been a famous fight. I did not believe him then, but I know now that he had hold of a tradition, and the king who fought there was not a George or a James, but Rufus, eight hundred years before. As I considered these things and other memories halting at this place, I came to wish that all history should be based upon legend. For the history of learned men is like a number of separate points set down very rare upon a great empty space, but the historic memories of the people are like a picture. They are one body whose distortion one can correct, but the mass of which is usually sound in stuff, and always in spirit.

Thinking these things I went down the hill with my companions, and I reoccupied my mind with the influence of that great and particular story of St. Thomas, whose shadow had lain over the whole of this road, until in these last few miles it had come to absorb it altogether.

The way was clear and straight like the flight of a bolt; it spanned a steep valley, passed a windmill on the height beyond, fell into the Watling Street (which here took on its alignment), and within a mile turned sharp to the south, crossed the bridge, and through the Westgate led us into Canterbury.

We had thoroughly worked out the whole of this difficult way. There stood in the Watling Street, that road of a dreadful antiquity, in front of a villa, an omnibus. Upon this we climbed, and feeling that a great work was accomplished, we sang a song. So singing, we rolled under the Westgate, and thus the journey ended.

There was another thing to be duly done before I could think my task was over. The city whose name and spell had drawn to itself all the road, and the shrine which was its core remained to be worshipped. The cathedral and the mastery of its central tower stood like a demand; but I was afraid, and the fear was just. I thought I should be like the men who lifted the last veil in the ritual of the hidden goddess, and having lifted it found there was nothing beyond, and that all the scheme was a cheat; or like what those must feel at the approach of death who say there is nothing in death but an end and no transition. I knew what had fallen upon the original soul of the place. I feared to find, and I found, nothing but stones.

I stood considering the city and the vast building and especially the immensity of the tower.

Even from a long way off it had made a pivot for all we saw; here closer by it appalled the senses. Save perhaps once at Beauvais, I had never known such a magic of great height and darkness.

SUCH A MAGIC OF GREAT HEIGHT AND DARKNESS

It was as though a shaft of influence had risen enormous above the shrine: the last of all the emanations which the sacred city cast outwards just as its sanctity died. That tower was yet new when the commissioners came riding in, guarded by terror all around them, to destroy, perhaps to burn, the poor materials of worship in the great choir below: it was the last thing in England which the true Gothic spirit made. It signifies the history of the three centuries during which Canterbury drew towards it all Europe. But it stands quite silent and emptied of every meaning, tragic and blind against the changing life of the sky and those activities of light that never fail or die as do all things intimate and our own, even religions. I received its silence for an hour, but without comfort and without response. It seemed only an awful and fitting terminal to that long way I had come. It sounded the note of all my road—the droning voice of extreme, incalculable age.

As I had so fixed the date of this journey, the hour and the day were the day and hour of the murder. The weather was the weather of the same day seven hundred and twenty-nine years before: a clear cold air, a clean sky, and a little wind. I went into the church and stood at the edge of the north transept, where the archbishop fell, and where a few Norman stones lend a material basis for the resurrection of the past. It was almost dark.... I had hoped in such an exact coincidence to see the gigantic figure, huge in its winter swaddling, watching the door from the cloister, watching it unbarred at his command. I had thought to discover the hard large face in profile, still caught by the last light from the round southern windows and gazing fixedly; the choir beyond at their alternate nasal chaunt; the clamour; the battering of oak; the jangle of arms, and of scabbards trailing, as the troops broke in; the footfalls of the monks that fled, the sharp insults, the blows and Gilbert groaning, wounded, and à Becket dead. I listened for Mauclerc's mad boast of violence, scattering the brains on the pavement and swearing that the dead could never rise; then for the rush and flight from the profanation of a temple, and for distant voices crying outside in the streets of the city, under the sunset, 'The King's Men! The King's!'

But there was no such vision. It seems that to an emptiness so utter not even ghosts can return.

In the inn, in the main room of it, I found my companions. A gramophone fitted with a monstrous trumpet roared out American songs, and to this sound the servants of the inn were holding a ball. Chief among them a woman of a dark and vigorous kind danced with an amazing vivacity, to the applause of her peers. With all this happiness we mingled.

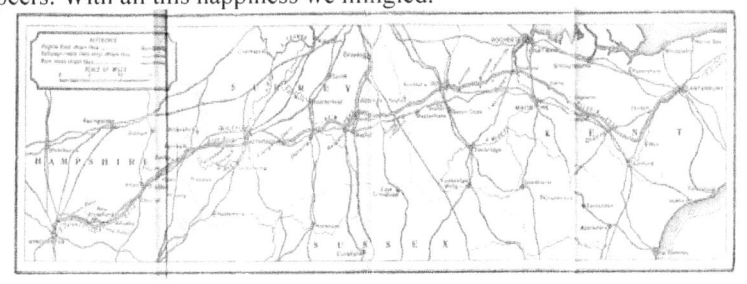

Made in the USA
Monee, IL
21 November 2022